CW01464973

SOUTH FROM BARLEY

The Story
of the
South Family
and
Samuel South & Sons
Horticultural Pottery Manufacturers

Kenneth Barker

Published by:
Kenneth Barker
64 Morris Way
London Colney
Herts. AL2 1JN

From whom further copies are available

For further information on the topics dealt with in this book please visit
http://www.samuelsouth.btinternet.co.uk

© Kenneth Barker 2006

ISBN 0 9553114 0 3

As from 1 January 2007 ISBN is changing to 13 digits as follows
ISBN 978 0 9553114 0 6

Printed by
Parchment the Printers
Printworks, Crescent Road
Cowley, Oxford, OX4 2PB

Front cover features the "Flowerpot Calendar" sent by Samuel South & Sons to their customers

"Anyone can throw bricks and pull things down but not everyone can build up"

"We are all so inclined to become immersed in business and trades that we are liable to lose sight of what is required of us citizens"

Samuel South(2) 1876-1956

Introduction

On 5 October 1960, the last hand thrown flowerpots were made at the White Hart Lane Potteries of Samuel South & Sons, a family business that had been founded by my great great grandfather, Joseph South, in 1868. The firm had been manufacturing on the site since 1886 and before that in Angel Road, Edmonton. Over the years, the South family had been also involved in brick-making, cartage and house-building. It seemed to me that there should be some record of these activities and the lives of the people involved before such memories and documents as survive became even more scattered amongst an already diverse family and lost forever.

The story begins in the small Hertfordshire villages of Barley, Barkway and Reed and follows the family migration southwards towards London and the establishment of their potteries in Edmonton and Tottenham. For some family members the southward journey continued even further, 13,000 miles away to New Zealand. It is, both historically and geographically, the story of South from Barley.

Ken Barker 2006

Note
Samuel was a popular name in the family. In order to avoid confusion the following suffixes have been used and, for the sake of uniformity, even in those circumstances in which the identity is apparent from the text.

Samuel South(1) 1853-1919 – son of Joseph South
Samuel South(2) 1876-1956 – son of Samuel(1)
Samuel South(3) 1908-1968 – son of Samuel(2)

Acknowledgements
Firstly, gratitude is owed to those members of the South family, now departed, who left records of their memories, in particular, Hilda Beech, Gladys Short, Samuel South(3), Charles South, Jim South and Joyce Barker. The following members of the family have provided valuable information, photographs and other memorabilia, Walter Barnard, Martin Beech, Jean Bowyer, Chris Haines, Maud Hickson, Roger Hickson, Brenda

Oddy, John Short, Michael Short, Christopher South, Eric South, Doris South, Graham South, Joan South and Peter South.

The story and aftermath of the emigration of Joseph South to New Zealand in 1874 relies heavily on the extensive research undertaken by his granddaughter, Judith Cranefield, who also provided much appreciated encouragement, constructive comment and an excellent proof reading service.

Kay Shekelton, Theresa Banfield, Bryan Long, Margaret Baker and Hazel Dunn supplied the Australian history. Tom Doig is responsible for the information about the Hertfordshire origins of the South family.

Thanks are due to Mr. A. W. Miller of Spigurnell Road, Tottenham, who interviewed Samuel South(3), Walter South and Sidney Cole in 1957 and deposited his detailed notes in the archives at Bruce Castle Museum. The assistance of the staff at the museum, Deborah Hedgcock, Jeff Gerhardt, Robert Waite, Libby Adams and Rita Read has been invaluable. Thanks also to Graham Dalling of Enfield Local History Unit, the staff at London Metropolitan Archives, House of Lords Record Office, British Telecom Archives and Marion Hyde of the Standard Gospel Library.

The history could not have been written without the help of Bert Brown, Nick Clark, Jim Clifton, Pat Cryer, Jim Deamer, Frank E. C. Forney, Roland Green, Chris Johnson, Ron Jones, Edith Knight, Dave Marden, Frank Marden, Bill Page, Albert Pinching, Julie Pegrum, Andy Porter, Christine Reed, Leslie Rodway, Peter Rooke, Bill Rust, Fred Stannard and Lyn Woodbridge.

With my sincere apologies for any inadvertent omissions.

Illustrations
The photographs and plans after page 54 are from the South Archive with exception of the 1895 Samuel South & Sons workforce which is reproduced by kind permission of Bruce Castle Museum.

Contents

Part 1 – The Family

Part 2 – The Potteries

Part One
The Family

Joseph South[1]
1822-1906

1822-1874

In north east Hertfordshire, close by the boundaries of Essex to the east and Cambridgeshire to the north, lie the villages of Reed, Barkway and Barley which, even today, remain unspoilt and retain their rural heritage. It was in these three villages, and surrounding settlements, that the recorded history of the South family begins. The first known ancestor, Edward Bysouth, was born in Reed about 1538 and the South line descended through his second son, also Edward.

The Bysouth and South surnames were interchangeable. Joseph Bysouth (b. 1608), the grandson of the first Edward, is recorded as either South or Bysouth as the whim seems to have taken him. His son, Richard, was baptised on 1 October 1654 and a note in the parish register records "out of the South cometh" presumably in explanation of possible confusion. The two surnames continued in usage but from the time of a later Joseph South (1790-1869) the South name alone was adopted. This later Joseph married Sarah Barnes and the union produced seven children, Samuel (b.1817), Benjamin (b.1821), Joseph (b.1822), John (b.1827), Henry (b.1830), Thomas (b.1832), and Sarah (b.1835). The modern history of the family begins with the third son, Joseph.

Over the generations most inhabitants of the villages were involved in the farming economy. For example, of the 870 persons recorded in the 1851 census for Barley, 574 were either farmers, farm labourers or their dependants. Jack Wilkerson in "Two Ears of Barley"[1] notes that when the demand for labour decreased men would leave their homes for several weeks and travel to districts to the north of London, such as Wood Green and Southgate, to cut hay for the local farmers. These farms supplied fodder for the large horse population of the capital. Perhaps a member of the South family made the journey to the area where, some years later, his descendants would settle.

On October 14 1844 Joseph South (b. 1822), then of Shaftoe End, Barley, married Emma Bright, a member of another long established local family, at the parish church of St. Margaret of Antioch. The marriage certificate records the occupation of Joseph as "Labourer (Brick Maker)" and that of his father-in-law, Henry, as a "Brickmaker". Both men were likely to have worked at the Morrice Green brickfield on the outskirts of Barley. Today evidence of the site of the brickfield is visible from the undulations of the ground and the locally produced bricks can be identified in the brickwork of buildings of that period. Whether it was Henry who introduced his son-in-law to the clay industry, in which the South family were to be engaged for five generations, must remain a matter for speculation.

The newly wed couple continued to live in Barley but after the birth of their first child, Ann, in 1847, Joseph started on his journey towards London. There were moves every two or three years to a new town or village before finally he settled in Edmonton, 30 miles to the south of Barley, in the 1850s. By the time their second daughter, Isabella, was born in 1848 the family had moved to the village of Standon, 10 miles from Barley, and his two sons, Joseph junior (b.1850) and Solomon (b. 1851),were born further south in Ware. Yet another move, and when Emma gave birth to Samuel(1) (b. 1853) they were residents of Cheshunt. However, by 1855, Joseph and Emma had crossed the boundary of Hertfordshire into the County of Middlesex and settled in Edmonton. Even after their arrival the family continued to move house, with addresses recorded in Church Lane, Fore Street and Angel Road. The remaining children, Clara (b.1855), Walter (b.1857), Keziah (b.1861), Arthur (b.1863) and Moses (b.1867) were born in the parish of Edmonton. There is evidence that Joseph maintained contact with his family during the journey southwards. For example, on the census night of the 30 March 1851 Joseph was living in Ware and his younger brother, John, together with two friends, William Lee and James Pettit,were visiting him.

A report "Wages and Earnings of the Working Classes" published in 1885[2] provides detailed information of the income and expenditure of working men and their families between 1857 and 1884. The period includes the time that Joseph (circa 1855-1874) lived in Edmonton and it is possible to obtain some indication of his financial status. In 1857 brickmakers were earning between 16s. [80p] and 20s. [£1] per week). Typically, earnings were insufficient to provide for a large family and reliance was placed on such other income that wives and children could earn. In the South household Joseph junior and Solomon were working in the brickfields at the ages of 10 and 9 respectively[3].

Over the next 30 years the wealth of the nation grew significantly and earnings increased by some 30%. Brickmakers now had weekly earnings from 21s. [£1.05] to 26s. [£1.30] and many staples had decreased in price, viz: butter, cheese, sugar, tea and rice. The improving economic situation enabled a working man to become his own master and to have savings. Once again, the national trend is reflected in the life of Joseph who, in 1868, established a small pottery, making flower pots, in Angel Road, Edmonton.

Edmonton was also the scene of some unhappy times for Joseph. Isabella died at the age of 6 in 1855 from a bout of pneumonia and in 1858 Clara, aged 2, succumbed to measles and a lung infection. Their mother was present at the deaths of both children. Emma, herself, contracted pulmonary tuberculosis ("phthisis") and died, aged 40, on 21 October 1868, the same year that Joseph had founded the small pottery. Little is known of Emma. She had lead a typical life for a woman of her class. Emma was probably illiterate, she had given birth to 10 children over 21 years, suffered the infant deaths of two of her daughters, raised a large family whilst moving frequently from village to village and, finally, died prematurely.

Emma's death left Joseph a widower with four of his children under the age of 11 to be cared for and brought up. But it was only ten months later, in August 1869, that he married again. Joseph was 47 and his new bride, Mary Ann Dutton, three months from her 20th birthday, was less than half his age. His eldest child, Ann aged 20, was older than her step-mother and the other older children were of a similar age, Joseph (18), Solomon (17), and Samuel (16). There is little doubt that family tensions were created.

Both Joseph and Mary Ann adhered to the Primitive Methodist faith which could provide a possible explanation for their acquaintance. Primitive Methodism was established in the 19th century by followers, led by Hugh Bourne, who considered that orthodox Methodism had strayed from the principles expounded by John Wesley. The movement was founded amongst the working class of the north of England and spread rapidly southwards. The movement continued as a separate entity until the two branches of Methodism were re-united in 1932.

It is possible that the South and Dutton families were known to each other through their common worship. It must be admitted that, at the present time, records of the Dutton family living in the Edmonton area have not been traced. If, however, the proposition of the prior acquaintance is correct then it is likely that Mary Ann came to help Joseph look after the younger children, perhaps, even moving in to live with the South family. The relationship between Joseph and Mary Ann grew closer and culminated in their marriage on 31 August 1868.

Direct evidence of family disagreements because of the marriage of Joseph and Mary Ann does not exist but there is circumstantial information that can be taken to support such a conclusion. For example, the wedding took place "out of area" at the parish church of St. Marylebone in central London with Joseph and Mary Ann giving their addresses as East Street and Clipstone Street respectively. Clipstone Street, W. 1 still exists and there was an East Street in Marylebone at the time. East Street, however, does not fit with Joseph's normal residency in Edmonton. An inference could be drawn that he established a temporary residency in order to qualify for marriage in a church away from Edmonton and his immediate family. If this was the case it suggests that the Clipstone Street address of Mary Ann was also temporary for if it was her family home there would have been no need for Joseph also to establish temporary residence because only one of the parties would need to live in the parish. On the other hand, if the Dutton family had lived Marylebone, the opportunity for meeting a member of the South family in the ordinary course of events would have been more remote.

Another consideration arising out of the marriage is that both Joseph and Mary Ann are registered as "of full age", that is to say, over 21, the age of consent. Joseph was certainly "of full age" but Mary Ann was born in November 1849 making her 19 at the time of the marriage. Marriages were often performed "out of area" if the bride was under 21 and marrying without the permission of her parents. However, Daniel Dutton, her father, was a witness so that consent, presumably, was not an issue. There is no satisfactory answer for Joseph marrying in St. Marylebone but it may be indicative of a wish to wed away from the Edmonton home and his family.

After their marriage Joseph and Mary Ann were living at 19 Angel Road, Edmonton, where their first son, Daniel, was born on 24 January, 1871 although he did not survive and died five weeks later suffering from "Convulsions". At the time Mary Ann registered the birth of their second child, Florence, on 29 September, 1873, her address was given as Frederick Place, Lower Fore Street, Edmonton.

Primitive Methodism was closely associated with the Victorian temperance movement which was supported by Mary Ann. On the evening of 28 November, 1871, the Band of Hope, a temperance organisation whose members signed a pledge of abstinence, held an entertainment of "Choruses, Melodies, Recitations, and Sacred Songs" at the Primitive Methodist Chapel in West Green, Tottenham[4]. Mrs. South (Mary Ann) performed "The Sister's Warning" and "Driven from Home". Her mother, Mrs. Dutton, took the chair. Other performances included "Catch the Sunshine", "I would like to be an Angel", "Intoxicating Drink" and "Watching for Pa". The poster advertising the event is most evocative, conjuring up the image of the audience sitting in a gas lit chapel on a cold November evening enjoying the sentimental and melodramatic Victorian entertainment. Doubtless Joseph was in the audience, perhaps with his younger children.

Emigration
By 1874 Joseph had reached the momentous decision to emigrate to New Zealand which involved a hazardous voyage of 13,000 miles to the other side of the world. Whether the decision was influenced by continuing family tensions brought about by the second marriage remains unproven. He was, however, well settled in his marriage to Mary Ann with their surviving child and the dependant children of his first marriage. He was the owner of the small pottery and economic necessity does not seem to have been a factor. The population of Edmonton and surrounding districts continued to expand and the demand for houses would require Joseph's brickmaking skills. In addition, the supply of flower pots to the nursery industry lasted for another 100 years. There seems to be no immediate reason, other than family conflict, for such a dramatic change in his life and

which resulted in the permanent separation from the members of his family who remained in the UK.

During the 19th Century there was substantial emigration from the UK primarily to the British Dominions of Australia, New Zealand, and Canada but also to the USA[1]. Between 1853 and 1913 almost 13 million emigrants left the UK and emigration to Australia and New Zealand was encouraged by assisted passages offered by the host country[2] and the creation of local emigration societies and funds in the UK. The National Emigration Aid Society was established in 1862 to lobby for grants from the UK government towards emigration and published an information sheet in 1869[3]. Details of assisted passages were provided including those available from the Province of Otago, in the South Island of New Zealand, which is reported as offering passages to Agricultural Labourers, Shepherds and Female Domestic Servants either on a payment of £7 or repayment of the sum six months after arrival. The unsubsidised steerage fare at the time was £15 to £19 dependant on the province concerned.

Emigration was not a new experience for the South family, three of Joseph's brothers, Benjamin, Henry and John, had left for Australia some twenty years before. After Joseph had married in 1844 and started on his journey southward to Edmonton his brothers, all labourers, remained in Barley. On census night, 30 March 1851, Benjamin, aged 30, and his wife, Fanny, were living in Shaf-toe End next door to his parents. Henry was in the High Street living with his wife, Sarah and in-laws. The third brother, John, was visiting Joseph in Ware leaving his wife, Sarah, and daughter, Emily, at home in Barley.

All three of the brothers jointly decided to emigrate to Australia and were attracted to the colony of Victoria in the south of the continent that was, at the time, experiencing the 1850s gold rush. In March 1853 they set sail with their wives and children on board the "Genghis Khan". Benjamin travelled on an assisted passage having arranged employment in Australia. John and Henry, without employment, made their own way. On arrival at Port Melbourne, Victoria, on 1 July 1853 Benjamin left to join his prospective employer and his two brothers and their families set off for the interior in bullock wagons. They settled in Maldon, a gold rush town in central Victoria.

At first the Souths occupied timber housing lined with canvas and furnished with wooden crates covered in cloth. During heavy rain specks of gold were washed into the street. John turned his hand to brickmaking and bricklaying. The gold rush had attracted a significant Chinese population and John constructed an ornamental brick oven in the local cemetery which was used to burn incense during their funerary rites. Now a listed building, the oven is a tourist attraction. One hundred and fifty years later the descendants of John and Henry continue to live in Maldon.

The three brothers, however, were not the first family migrants. A year earlier, an uncle, James Bysouth, who was a widower, left England with the two youngest of his six children. After a long voyage of nearly 4½ months James disembarked at Geelong, Victoria, on 12 December 1852. He was employed as an agricultural worker in the district of Indented Heads and later became a drover. In the following years James married again and two of his elder sons joined him in Australia.

Why did Joseph select Dunedin in the province of Otago, New Zealand, as his destination? Australia, with the presence of close members of his family, surely must have been considered a possible destination once the decision to emigrate had been made. The 1851 census is evidence that he kept in contact with his brothers after leaving Barley. At these meetings, presumably, the topic of emigration could well have been discussed bearing in mind that Benjamin, John and Henry departed only two years later. The information provided by the passenger list of the "Genghis Khan" confirms that both John and Henry and their wives were literate and could have written to their relatives with news of their experiences.

Dunedin, in the South Island of New Zealand, was one of the more distant places inviting immigration. Shortly after his arrival, Joseph established a brickmaking business which suggests some knowledge that suitable clay was available and a ready market for bricks existed. At the time there was a demand for bricks in Otago and official reports were prepared in 1875 and 1879 concerning the possibilities for improvements in brickmaking and the suitability of the local clays in Otago. Both reports received publicity in the UK but, of course, were too late to have influenced Joseph in his decision.

Whatever the reason for his chosen destination, it is most unlikely that it had been a random decision.

Joseph and his family travelled on an assisted passage to New Zealand. Advertisements offering such passages appeared in newspapers and agents were appointed in the UK to promote the assisted schemes and process suitable applicants. Character references and medical certificates witnessed by a clergyman or magistrate were required.

The Voyage[1]
In the weeks before departure Joseph made preparations for the voyage, not least of which was the sale of the pottery to his son, Samuel(1). On the journey to New Zealand Joseph was accompanied by Mary Ann and their daughter, Florence, together with the younger children of the first marriage, Walter, Keziah, Arthur and Moses. Mary Ann was pregnant with her third child, Cordelia. The older children from the marriage to Emma, Ann, Joseph (both of whom were married), Solomon and Samuel(1) remained in the UK.

The standards of safety and accommodation on board emigrant ships at the time varied and, on occasion, they were the subject of official concern and investigation. Fire and the spread of disease, especially among the more vulnerable younger children, were the greatest fears. The dangers were demonstrated when in September 1874, six months after Joseph left the UK, the "Cospatrick" caught fire on the voyage to New Zealand and all 429 immigrants perished. Because of the long voyage involved, the New Zealand authorities imposed stricter health and safety regulations governing ships chartered to transport immigrants.

Joseph was fortunate in the choice of ship that had been chartered for the voyage. The "Buckinghamshire" was a new, iron hulled, twin decked ship built six years earlier in 1868 by Barclay, Curtis & Co[2]. of Glasgow having "lofty, well lighted and well ventilated 'tween decks" and "a roomy main deck"[3]. Equipment included a condenser for the production of fresh water during the voyage and the vessel was "capitally appointed throughout"[4]. The ship had an overall length of 282 feet, a breadth of 37.5 feet and a tonnage of 1466 tons[5]. According to Lloyd's Registry of Shipping, the vessel was constructed to a higher specification than the current regulations demanded.

Typically, accommodation for steerage passengers on assisted passages was provided on the lower deck with separate accommodation for single men (forward) and single women (aft) under the supervision of a matron. Bunks lined the sides of the deck and the central area was used for living, eating and all other activities. The cramped conditions frequently caused tensions when the passengers were confined to their quarters because of bad weather, sometimes for several days. Boys over the age of 12 travelling with their families were transferred to the single male accommodation for the duration of the voyage. Medical facilities were provided on board with a Surgeon Superintendent in attendance. The "Buckinghamshire" was under the command of Captain Robert Harland, an experienced mariner[6].

The South family and the other emigrants bound for New Zealand boarded the "Buckinghamshire", which was berthed in the East India Docks, London, on the 4 March 1874. 505 passengers embarked comprising families, single men and single women primarily from the south of England and, particularly, from Middlesex. There was a wide range of occupations declared by the skilled men and a large proportion of labourers. Joseph was described as a brickmaker from Hertfordshire although he had been living in Edmonton, Middlesex, and the passenger list also reveals other incorrect information concerning his domestic affairs. He adopted the name of his younger brother, Henry, and provided false age details for himself, Mary Ann, Walter,Keziah and Arthur:

Name	Age on Passenger List	Date of Birth	Age in March 1874
Henry [Joseph]	44	24/11/1822	52
Mary Ann	42	29/11/1849	24
Walter	14	3/9/1857	16
Keziah	11	23/12/1860	13
Arthur	9	13/11/1863	10
Moses	7	1867	7
Florence	4 months	29/9/1873	5 months

Four days later, on 8 March 1874, the "Buckinghamshire" sailed from its berth and moved slowly down river before stopping at Gravesend to send stowaways ashore and to take on board cabin passengers who had paid the full fare. Traditionally, the route taken on the voyage to New Zealand took the ship south west across the Atlantic before making a wide sweep around the Cape of Good Hope into the "roaring forties"; the trade winds that assisted the ship's headway.

Three weeks after setting sail the "Buckinghamshire" crossed the equator on 3 April. The weather remained fine but a heavy gale one night broke off part of the jib boom which was carried away. In the stormy weather, as they approached the Cape of Good Hope, a sailor fell overboard but he was rescued. The weather became increasingly unsettled and cold. In the heavy gales and rough seas waves were breaking over the ship, the top gallant yard was snapped in half and the single women's quarters were swamped. Passengers were battened down below deck. The enforced confinement caused tempers to rise amongst the passengers. Hail, snow and piercing winds buffeted the ship for four weeks. The weather improved in the second half of May as the ship neared Tasmania. After anchoring off the Heads of the Otago Harbour, the pilot came on board and the "Buckinghamshire" was towed into Port Chalmers, the seaport of Dunedin, and anchored on 28 May 1874.

The ship carried no infectious diseases[7] and was not required to be quarantined but, nonetheless, lay at anchor for nearly a week because there was no room in the immigration barracks. A journalist from the Otago Witness reporting on the arrival of the "Buckinghamshire" was impressed with the newly arrived immigrants and reported that they "appeared to be above the average of respectability, and were clean and tidy in person"[8].

The trials and tribulations of the voyage experienced by the South family and their fellow passengers were typical of those endured by migrants to New Zealand. There had been four deaths, two births and a stillbirth amongst the passengers during the journey. Mary Ann, pregnant with her third child, and with four other children, including a baby of four months, had coped with the crowded, noisy and smelly conditions below deck, the cold and the seasickness. But the family were now set to establish themselves in their new home country.

1874-1906

Joseph and Mary Ann settled well into their new life in Dunedin and became respected members of their church community. Mary Ann was particularly active in local affairs being a member of several local societies and became President of the local branch of the Women's Christian Temperance Movement. Her parents had followed their daughter to New Zealand in 1875 and later her sister arrived. The family continued to increase with the birth of Cordelia (b. 1874), Cornelius (b. 1877), Ernest (b. 1878), Evangeline (b. 1880), Henry (b. 1882), Emalene (b. 1885) and Elizabeth who was born in 1889 when Joseph was 67.

Within a few months after his arrival in New Zealand Joseph had opened a brickfield in the Anderson's Bay area of Dunedin and later expanded the business with further works in Walton Park, Fairfield, on land leased from the government. Both branches of "South & Sons" continued to trade until the Anderson's Bay operation was closed in 1891. History repeated itself when, in August 1901, Joseph, now aged 79, sold the plant, machinery and stock of the business, together with the lease to his son, Ernest, for the sum of £115 16s. 6d. A stock of 1000 "Flower Pots" was included in the inventory suggesting that there was also an involvement with potmaking. The purchase was arranged by a down payment of £15 16s. 6d. and the balance by four equal payments of £25 over the following 12 months. Unlike the sale of his Edmonton pottery to Samuel, on this occasion two horses were included in the transaction. Ernest continued to manage the business until its closure in 1906.

Joseph died on 20 December 1906 aged 84. He had experienced an eventful life. Firstly, he moved away from his birthplace where his ancestors had lived for many generations and, later, went on an epic voyage to settle on the other side of the world. The pottery business that he founded in 1868 was continued by his descendants for a further 92 years and, on arrival in New Zealand, he went on to establish a second enterprise. In his personal life, Joseph suffered the unhappiness of the premature death of his first wife and the infant deaths of three of the nineteen children from his two marriages. His widow, Mary Ann, remarried eight years later and died in 1916.

Children[1]

The marriage of Joseph South and Emma Bright produced ten children. Two of their daughters, Isabella (1848-1855) and Clara (1855-1858), died in infancy. When Joseph emigrated in 1874, the four adult children, Ann, Joseph, Solomon and Samuel(1) stayed behind in the UK and the younger members of the family, Walter, Keziah, Arthur and Moses accompanied their father and step-mother on the long voyage to New Zealand.

Details of the children of his second marriage are given in Appendix 1.

Ann South 1847-1898

Ann (also known as Annie), the eldest child of Joseph and Emma, was baptised at Barley on St Stephen's Day, 26 December 1847. She accompanied her parents on the moves southward until their arrival in Edmonton in the 1850s and by 1861 was living with them in Church Lane. Ann was 20 when her mother, Emma, died in October 1868. Her marriage to William Passaway took place five months later on 28 March 1869 and in August of the same year Joseph married again. His new bride, Mary Ann Dutton, aged 19, was younger than her step-daughter.

William and Ann married in the Parish Church of West Hackney and both gave that district as their place of residence. Residence in Hackney is unexpected because the available records show that, in the years before the wedding, Ann and her family had lived in Edmonton whilst William was an inhabitant of Tottenham. After the marriage the couple returned to Tottenham and lived there continuously until Ann's death in 1898[1].

By the time that Joseph emigrated to New Zealand in March 1874 Ann was the mother of three children and gave birth to her fourth child the following month. She remained in the UK along with her brothers, Joseph, Solomon and Samuel(1) and a close relationship continued between them. Ann's son, John (b. 1879), was employed as a potter between 1893-1914 whilst he was living at addresses in Tottenham and Wood Green[2]. It is most likely that he was working for his uncle, Samuel(1), at the White Hart Lane Potteries.

Earlier, Emma Passaway, the younger sister of William, had been a witness at the marriage of Joseph South junior and Sarah Webb in 1870. Two members of the Passaway family, possibly a son and daughter of Ann and William, have been identified amongst the guests in the group photograph taken at the wedding of Samuel South(2) and Emily Maud King in September 1899[3]. A Mr. Pass[a]way is listed as a mourner in the main procession attending the 1919 funeral of Samuel South(1)[4].

William Passaway was a labourer at the time of the marriage to Ann later taking up the occupation of house painter and decorator[5]. The first of their ten children, William, was born in Edmonton and by 1871 the family was living in Princes Street, Tottenham, then moving a few streets away to 8 Beaufoy Road and later 9 Beaufoy Road[6] where Ann died on 26 December 1898, the 51st anniversary of her baptism.

Joseph South 1850-1897

Joseph South, the eldest son of Joseph and Emma South, was born in 1850 whilst the family were living in Ware, Hertfordshire. At the age of 10 Joseph was working in an Edmonton brickfield, presumably, with his father. His mother, Emma, died in 1868 when Joseph was eighteen and the following year his father married again. However, his stepmother, Mary Ann Dutton, aged 19, was of a similar age to himself. In 1870 Joseph married Sarah Webb who had been born in Braughing, a small village between Barley, his father's birthplace, and Ware. His sister-in-law,Emma Passaway,was a witness and the marriage produced two children, Eliza Emily (b. 1871) and Florence Ellen (b. 1874).

Joseph junior remained in the UK with his older sister, Ann, and younger brothers Solomon and Samuel(1) when his father emigrated to New Zealand in March 1874. Before departing, Joseph sold his Angel Road Pottery to Samuel(1) bypassing his eldest son and perhaps indicative of a family rift. At the registration of the birth of his second daughter in October 1874 Joseph(2) declared his occupation as Brickmaker and Potter"and that the birth took place at his residence "The Pottery, Angel Road [Edmonton]". The Edmonton Rating register for 1878 has Joseph as the registered occupier of the dwelling and land in Angel Road and, as late as 1884, he continues to be recorded as the recognised occupier of the "Cottage, stables and Pot Manufactory" although the cottage was then occupied by his parents-in-law and their son, William.

By 1878, however, Joseph had moved to Fore Street, Edmonton, and seems to have severed his connection with the pottery in order to further his own career. Within three years, in the 1881 census, Joseph declares his occupation as "Carman and Contractor employing 9 men 1 boy". From subsequent records it is reasonable to assume that the contracting arm of his business was concerned with house building in Edmonton.

In 1890 Joseph, in partnership with John Edmondson, bought two building plots at the junction of Brettenham Road and Felixstowe Road, Edmonton[1]. Later, the developed sites were sold separately. Nos. 1-7 Brettenham Road with the "dwelling houses lately erected by the Vendor" were sold in 1893 to Elisabeth Kencher[2] and the remaining developed land, nos. 1-7 Felixstowe Road to Alfred Cox, a London solicitor, in 1894[3]. During the 1890s 17 houses, known as St. Peter's Terrace, Grosvenor Road[4], and 14 houses, nos. 1-27 Chester Road[5], were also built and sold by Joseph. Not all houses were sold with the freehold. In 1892 he was the owner of 21 houses in Brettenham Road (Rose Terrace) and further 19 houses in Edinburgh Road which would have provided a rental income[6].

In his private life Joseph achieved some standing in the local religious community. Not only was he a trustee of the Primitive Methodist Chapels in Enfield[7] and West Green Road, Tottenham[8] but he was also a regular communicant[9] at the Congregational Church in Snells Park, Edmonton, where his nephew, Samuel South(2) was to marry in 1899. His younger daughter, Florence, was noted for her fine solo singing at the church[10]. The extent of his spiritual commitment was exemplified by the presence of ministers of different denominations at his funeral.

In addition to his house building activities, by the 1890s, Joseph was operating a brickfield on 13 acres of land to the north of Bury Street, Edmonton. It was as a result of an apparently minor accident at the brickfield that Joseph met his premature death at the age of 47[11]. On 26 January 1897 Joseph left home in Fore Street as usual and walked to the brickfield. The weather was cold and there had been a heavy frost. During the course of the morning Joseph was walking across the brickfield with William Webb, his foreman and brother-in-law, when he stumbled on the hard ground and twisted his leg. Later, he began to feel unwell and returned home by tram arriving in the early afternoon. He told his wife, Sarah, about the accident and went to lay down. The following day, Joseph went to the brickfield but was again obliged to return home. He consulted his doctor the same day and thereafter daily home visits were made. His condition did not improve and Joseph died a month later on the 25 February 1897.

At the inquest held on Saturday 27 February his doctor, Dr. Green, gave evidence that he had diagnosed a sprain or slight tear of the muscle as a result of the incident at the brickfield. He concluded that a blood clot had formed at the seat of the injury, become detached and caused an obstruction to the pulmonary artery. The Coroner accepted the medical evidence and a verdict of Accidental Death was returned.

The funeral took place on 3 March 1897. Shops and houses in Fore Street, on the route of the cortege, had their blinds drawn. Members of the Council and local businessmen, including fellow brickmakers, were amongst the mourners. There was a distinct ecumenical presence. The service was conducted by the Rev. T. Bagley, a Congregationalist minister, and the Rev. R. Cornell, former minister of the Northumberland Park Primitive Methodist Chapel. Ministers from the local Anglican Church and Baptist Chapel were also in attendance. Joseph was interred at Edmonton Cemetery, and, over the coming years, other family members would be buried in neighbouring plots.

His entire estate, with a probate value of £3,974, was left to his widow, Sarah. The following year, Sarah, now aged 47, sold the brickfield to Joseph's younger brother, Samuel[12]. By the time of the 1901 Census, she had moved to Northumberland Park in Tottenham where she lived with her unmarried daughter, Emily, and next door to the younger daughter, Florence, who had married a freelance journalist, Albert Rix. Her independent means enabled both Sarah and her daughter to live without additional earnings from employment and to enjoy the services of a live-in maid. Sarah died in 1910.

Joseph South, who had started work at the age of 10, had become a successful businessman and respected member of the community entirely by his own efforts. By the time the Edmonton brickfield had been established, his brother, Samuel(1), was expanding his own interests at the White Hart Lane Potteries. Sibling rivalry can be imagined between the two brothers, each anxious to demonstrate his own success to the other. Sadly, Joseph's own future ambitions were cut short.

Solomon South 1851-1926
Solomon, the fourth child and second son, was born on 9 November 1851 whilst the South family were living in Westmill Road, Ware. By 1861, after the family had moved to Edmonton, he was working in a brickfield with his father. Solomon was 17 when Joseph remarried in 1869 after the death of his first wife, Emma, the previous year. The 1871 census finds Solomon serving as a driver in the Royal Artillery and stationed at the "Royal Horse Infirmary and Military Camp Huts and Remount Establishment" on Woolwich Common.

He was no longer in the army when he married Eliza Berndes in March 1881. His father-in-law, Henry, was an immigrant having been born in Westphalia, Prussia. The newly-weds set up home in Sutherland Road, Edmonton, next door to Henry Berndes and his family. There were at least seven children of the marriage, Alfred, Henry, Mabel, May, Elsie, Walter and Florrie. Solomon was employed in various capacities by his brothers, Joseph and Samuel(1) and in the census and registration certificates he is variously described as a brickmaker, earthman – flower pot maker, labourer – potteries and foreman horse keeper.

Solomon outlived his siblings Ann, Joseph and Samuel(1). He is listed amongst the official mourners at the 1919 funeral of his brother, Samuel(1)[1]. His own death from bronchial asthma and a heart condition occurred in January 1926.

Samuel South(1) 1853-1919
The history of Samuel South(1) is dealt with separately (see page 18).

Walter South 1857-
Walter was 16 at the time of his father's emigration and on board the "Buckinghamshire" he would have travelled in the single men's accommodation separated from his family. At first, Walter worked in the brickfield established by his father but, later, after his marriage to Annie Luke, he moved to Sydney, Australia. Walter maintained contact, however,

not only with his family in New Zealand but also with the relatives left behind in England. Children: Olive, Walter, Annie, Harold, Jim.

Jeanette Keziah South 1860 -1935
As the eldest daughter of the children who emigrated, Keziah helped her step-mother with her younger brothers. In 1880 she married Thomas Clarkson an immigrant from Scotland who died six years later in 1886 leaving the young widow to raise four children. Little is known of her life but there was a struggle to provide for her family. Keziah lived to the age of 72 and died in 1935. Children: Thomas, Frederick, Maude, Jack.

Arthur South 1863-
Arthur started work at his father's brickfield at Anderson's Bay and, later, managed the second brickworks that had been established in Walton Park, Fairfield. By 1891 he had married Mary Daly and opened a milliners and dyers business in central Dunedin. Later still he worked as a hairdresser in Dunedin and moved to the North Island in 1917. Children: Arthur, Herbert, Helena.

Moses South 1867-1949
Moses was the tenth child of the first marriage and was born in the year before his mother died. In New Zealand, he stayed on at school after completing primary education in order to work as a Pupil Teacher for four years. In this way he qualified for entry to Dunedin Teachers' Training College. Leaving before the two year course was complete he taught at two South Island country schools one in a very remote mining settlement. Marrying Emma Dodds in Dunedin he worked briefly as a hairdresser until his wife's poor health at the time made him decide to move to a warmer climate. Moses transferred to the Native School Service and they sailed to the extreme north of New Zealand where they both taught at an isolated native school at Whangape for five years before moving south to the Nuhaka Native School in Hawkes Bay. Moses became a greatly respected leader in Native School education and in the local Maori Community. All his life he was active in the Presbyterian Church, taking services in the absence of a Minister and in his retirement, becoming a Church Elder. He was a fine musician, playing the trumpet and excelling with school bands and choirs. Children: Laurie, Leslie, Joyce, Muriel.

Samuel South(1)
1853-1919

1853-1919

Samuel South(1), the fourth child, of Joseph and Emma South was born in 1853 while the South family were living in Cheshunt, Hertfordshire, and before they finally moved to Edmonton in the County of Middlesex. At an early age, he started working in the brickfields with his father. A significant disruption in his life happened when Samuel(1) was 16. His mother died in 1868 and the following year his father married Mary Ann Dutton who was 19 years old. The age of their step mother is thought to have created tensions with the older children of the first marriage and, a few years later, in 1874 Joseph and Mary Ann emigrated to New Zealand taking Samuel(1)'s younger brothers and sisters with them. Before his departure, Joseph sold the small pottery he had established in Angel Road, Edmonton, to Samuel(1).

On 25 July 1875 Samuel(1) married Alice Barnard at All Hallows Church, Tottenham. The newly wed couple moved into a modest house, 26 Angel Road Terrace, Edmonton, which was close to the pottery that he now owned. Seven of his children, Samuel(2) (b. 1876), Alice (b. 1878), Emily (b. 1880), Walter (b. 1881), John (b. 1883), Ethel (b.1884), and Arthur (b. 1886), were born in Edmonton but in 1886 Samuel(1) transferred his pottery business to a much larger site in White Hart Lane, Tottenham, and by 1891 the family had moved to Tentdale. Tentdale was a pair of cottage properties located on the east side of the entrance to E. G. Cole & Son, a rival potmaker occupying the land adjacent to the South pottery. Their new home provided more accommodation for the growing South family and comprised two storeys and a third attic floor in the mansard roof. Samuel(1) occupied the eastern half of the property and the Cole family lived next door. The last of his ten children, Charles (b. 1889), Alfred (b. 1891) and Lilly (b. 1894), were born at Tentdale.

For a short period towards the end of the 1890s Samuel(1) was living at Devonshire Hill Farm[1] leased from the New River Company. The farmhouse lay to the north of the pottery with the farmland extending westwards to Wolves Lane. Accommodation comprised hall, dining and drawing rooms, 2 parlours, kitchen and washhouse on the ground floor with access to the cellar, 4 bedrooms on the first floor and a further 4 rooms in the upper attic floor[2]. An ornamental garden to the rear of the house led to a footbridge across the abandoned channel of the New River which remained in water at that time[3]. There were two further cottages and a wide range of outbuildings including a coach house, stables, piggery and barns[4]. By 1901, however, Samuel(1) had moved yet again but the lease of Devonshire Hill Farm was retained with the dwellings rented out. The farm land was used for pasture and hay fields providing fodder for the pottery horses.

In 1901 Samuel(1) was occupying Langhedge House, 43 Snells Park, Edmonton, where he lived for the remainder of his life. Snells Park is one of three roads forming an inverted triangle off Fore Street immediately to the north of the boundary with Tottenham. Langhedge Lane and Snells Park diverge from the southern "apex" at the junction with Fore Street and connected by Grove Street at the northern "base" of the triangle. The housing estate was formerly the site of a large house and grounds occupied by Nathaniel Snell and sold for housing development in 1848/49. There had been an effort to provide varied accommodation with a mixture of smaller terraced housing, semi-detached villas and detached houses. The impressive Gothic style Tottenham and Edmonton Congregational Church stood at the southern entrance to the estate and St. James Church of England School was located at the northern end. With the corner shop and Grove Public House, easy access to the nearby shops in Fore Street and Tottenham High Road, Snells Park was a self contained community.

Langhedge House was a double-fronted detached house on the west side of Snells Park with a 50 ft. frontage to the road. The house was a fitting residence for the successful business man that Samuel(1) had now become. Accommodation consisted of three living rooms, kitchen, scullery, larder and wash-house to the ground floor, four first floor bedrooms, a bathroom on a half landing and an attic[5]. Large paintings in gilt frames adorned the walls[6]. The dining room was furnished with a large table, 9ft. 6in. by 4ft. 6in.[7] around which the family would gather for their meals. Extending some 200 ft., the well kept garden, decorated with ornamental pots and urns[8], gave access to Langhedge Lane[9]. Prize chrysanthemums were grown in two greenhouses. The gardener employed by Samuel(1) forbade the visiting grandchildren to enter these[10].

At the time of the move to Snells Park, Samuel(1) was the owner of pottery, brickmaking and cartage businesses and was also becoming a not insubstantial property owner. He had acquired the brickfield in 1898 from his brother's widow[11] and developed the cartage operation with the horses used to deliver the bricks and pots to customers. Advertisements for Samuel South & Sons proudly proclaimed "Cartage Contractors, Horticultural Garden Pots and Brick Manufacturers".

Snells Park was (comparatively) much further from the White Hart Lane Potteries than Devonshire Hill Farm. The new home, however, was about mid-way between the pottery and the brickfield so that access to both of his businesses was easier. Previous properties had been either rented or leased but there was the opportunity to acquire the freehold of 43 Snells Park which was purchased by Samuel(1) in 1908[12]. In addition, the house was close to his chosen place of worship.

In 1892, aged 39, Samuel(1) had been admitted as a member of the Strict Baptist Ebenezer Chapel in Claremont Road, off Fore Street, less than 5 minutes walk from his Snells Park home[13]. Strict Baptists had split from the main body of the faith because of doctrinal differences and the worshippers at Claremont Road have been described as "a very extreme group" and "although individually they may be inestimable in character, yet their creed is severe"[14]. The chapel was a simple building, erected in 1818 (and demolished in 1959), with room for a congregation of 150 members[15]. Services were austere with extempore prayers[16] and unaccompanied hymns, the pitch being given with a tuning fork[17]. Despite his late admission Samuel(1) went on to be elected Trustee, Deacon and Treasurer of the Chapel[18]. A fellow member of the congregation was Joshua Pedley, a wealthy solicitor and local benefactor, who lived in Trafalgar House, a substantial property in White Hart Lane, Tottenham[19]. He was the senior partner of Pedley, May & Fletcher who acted for the South family until the death of Samuel South(2) in 1956 and provided finance by the way of mortgages for many of their property transactions.

Visiting circuit preachers sometimes stayed at the Snells Park home[20]. On these occasions a hanging picture of a woman, with her shoulders uncovered, was politely turned to face the wall[21]. A similar sensitivity about appropriate attire was shown when he reprimanded one of his daughters for walking from her bedroom onto the landing wearing her chemise[22]. Family prayers were held at home which his sons sometimes tried to avoid by hiding in the lavatory[23]. Samuel(1) forbade his children to drink, smoke or play cards. When Samuel(2) and his family moved to 39 Snells Park in 1908, his five younger brothers called frequently upon their married brother in order to indulge in these pastimes[24].

Despite their strict upbringing, his sons had a sense of fun[25]. On being told by their father that whilst any fool can sing at night, it takes a man to sing in the morning, the sons rose early the next day and sang loudly outside their parents' bedroom[26]. Whilst living at Tentdale, the boys had helped a local farmer to round up some of his pigs that had escaped[27]. The farmer rewarded them with sixpence and, later, the boys released the pigs themselves anxious to benefit once again. Their prank was discovered and they received a punishment rather than a reward. One November, at Tentdale, they were surprised when their father produced a box of fireworks to celebrate "Guy Fawkes night". Samuel(1) took charge and issued many admonitions to *"Keep back, you boys!"*. He succeeded, however, in setting fire to the whole box much to the amusement of his sons. Especially as an errant firework set light to the ivy covered outside privy.

His four daughters, however, seem to have been subject to a greater degree of control than the sons. The eldest, Alice, and, youngest, Lily, never married. Ethel was 27 when she married Gordon Smith, owner of a men's outfitters, in 1911 and it was not until 1927 that Emily, aged 47, married George Sayer, a widower.

In March 1904 Samuel(1) stood as a candidate for the Ratepayers' and Traders Defence Association at the elections for the Edmonton District Council, Fore Street Ward [28]. Twenty-one candidates offered themselves for election including a fellow brick maker, W. D. Cornish[29]. Samuel(1) was an unsuccessful candidate receiving 343 votes but the Ratepayers Association became the majority party on the Council[30].

A report of polling day in the local newspaper[31] describes scenes not experienced in today's apathetic attitude towards local elections:

"The excitement of the elections was mostly concentrated in the last three hours. Everybody who was anybody for this particular occasion was about. Candidates and their friends who had been unable to forego their daily toil now appeared on the scene, and the knots of men and women and boys at the polling places grew larger and more excited, and the noise increased in volume...................Darkness closed in upon a busy scene. Motors and all manner of vehicles, from smart carriages to a humble and a somewhat dilapidated looking van, travelled to and from the railway stations and up and down the streets ....Ratepayers and Progressives were both well off for conveyances ....although the Socialists could only boast one or two...... It would be difficult to have found a more lively spot .....than the Lower Edmonton railway station. Hundreds of people collected there, and the efforts to induce the travellers to "jump up" made a curious and interesting spectacle....... In the final hour the strain on the polling stations was very considerable...... the doors were shut, and so many people were admitted at a time"

Samuel(1) may well have been amongst the throng with the horse and trap which he used to travel between his businesses. In 1903 the horse, that he kept in a field near Montague Road, Edmonton, was stolen[32]. At 10 p.m., the culprit, George Dobbs, took the horse to a local slaughterer explaining that the "old man" wanted the animal slaughtered. Because of the late hour, the explanation raised the suspicions of the slaughterman who reported the incident to the police. Dobbs appeared at Middlesex Sessions in July 1903 and was sentenced to 18 months hard labour.

In his later years Samuel(1) was typically attired in a dark morning coat and a "truncated" top hat[33]. His grandchildren[34] have described him as a severe and austere man who they held in great awe although, perhaps, allowance should be made for the perception of elderly adults by young children. There is evidence that, in his sixties, Samuel(1) was considering a visit to his younger brothers and sister who had emigrated to New Zealand with their father in 1874[35]. Having travelled to the USA in 1911 and the Continent in 1914 the longer voyage involved is unlikely to have caused him too much concern. By 1914 his younger brother, Walter, together with his family, had moved from New Zealand to Australia and was living in Sydney. That same year, Samuel(1)'s niece, Gertrude Burren nce Passaway, the daughter of his sister, Ann, was residing with Walter having travelled from the UK to Australia. Gertrude brought all the family news from England, especially of Samuel(1), and informed Walter that he was thinking of a visit. The outbreak of the First World War would have put paid to such plans and, after the cessation of hostilities, Samuel(1) died within two months of the Armistice. Gertrude's husband, James, had enlisted in the Royal Australian Navy and was lost at sea in 1918[36].

On Wednesday 1 January 1919 Samuel(1) travelled from Snells Park to the White Hart Lane Potteries[37]. Samuel(2) thought that his father looked unwell and enquired after his health. Samuel(1) replied that *"I don't feel quite up to it, boy.* He remained in the pottery office but during the course of the morning his condition worsened and he was taken home in the horse and trap. Overnight, Samuel(1) died in his sleep. At the subsequent inquest the medical evidence disclosed that there was an enlargement of the heart and that death had resulted from an aneurism. A verdict of natural causes was entered.

A wide circle of and family, friends and business acquaintances attended the funeral on Friday 10 January 1919[38]. The hearse was followed by six carriages which conveyed the official mourners followed by many representatives of the nursery, potmaking and brickmaking industries including his rival potmaker and neighbour, Edward Cole . His son, Alfred, serving in France, was unable to be present. The minister of the Strict Baptist Chapel, Manor Park, conducted the service at the graveside and Samuel was interred at Edmonton Cemetery in a plot next to the grave of his brother, Joseph. His widow, Alice, with her three unmarried daughters moved to a South Estate house in Mount Pleasant Road, Tottenham, where she lived until her own death in 1936, aged 87.

Samuel South(1) typified the Victorian ideals of rectitude, self-reliance and improvement. Having overcome the personal unhappiness that would have arisen from the premature death of his mother and emigration of his father, and with little formal education, he developed the small pottery founded by his father into a successful business enterprise that, at various times, embraced brickmaking, cartage, local authority contracting, property and land ownership.

Brickmaking
On 2 March 1894 in partnership with Charles Hastings, Samuel(1) entered a short term agreement with the landowner, John Edward Ford, to lease a field of seven acres to the north of White Hart Lane for the purposes of brickmaking[1]. The field was located some 200 hundred yards east of the

South pottery and was part of a much larger area of land which Samuel(1) was to purchase in 1912. Under the contract John Ford received a:

"surface rental of Two shillings and sixpence and a Royalty of Two shillings and sixpence on Ten hundred thousand Bricks at least whether so many Bricks are made or not and the same Royalty of Two shillings and sixpence per thousand on any further or greater quantity that any be made".

A period of 3 months was allowed for the removal of bricks from the site after expiry of the agreement on 1 November 1894.

By the final decade of the nineteenth century his brother, Joseph South junior, in addition to his own contracting and house building activities, was the owner of a brickfield off Bury Street, Lower Edmonton, which overlaid a belt of brickearth. The 13 acre site was acquired in two parcels from members of the Bowles family. In 1890, the first 6 acres were purchased, in partnership with John Edmondson,[2] and the field extended in 1896 when the remaining 7 acres were acquired[3]. Rights of way "with or without horses" to Bury Street in the south and Hertford Road to the east were included in the conveyances. Two other brickmakers, Cornish and Plowman, occupied adjoining land to the north of the South brickfield[4].

Joseph died prematurely in 1897 at the age of 47 after a fall at the brickfield and his widow, Sarah, inherited his entire estate[5]. The following year Sarah decided to sell the brickfield to her brother-in-law, Samuel South(1)[6], who financed the purchase with the assistance of a mortgage provided by partners of his solicitors, Pedley, May & Fletcher[7]. Samuel South & Sons were members of the North & East London Brick Masters Association of Upper Edmonton, a business association of local brickmakers which, amongst their interests, agreed rates of pay and set the price of bricks[8]. Many years later, in 1937, Samuel South(2) addressed the Rotary Club of Wood Green. He recalled that there were about twenty brickmakers at the turn of the century and went on to say *"I used to make myself unpopular at these meetings but managed to stop the time wasting by proposing that we put a shilling on every thousand bricks. Better times were in store for the industry and the men in it after that"[9].*

There was a ready local market for the bricks manufactured at the brickfield. A grandson of Samuel(1) has recalled when alterations were being carried out to a house owned by South Brothers bricks were discovered with the stamp "SSS" – Samuel South & Sons[10]. Brickmaking ceased, however, shortly before the outbreak of the first world war and the last reference in the Kelly's directory for the district appeared in the 1911-1912 edition.

The land is now a recreation ground and the boundaries precisely follow the former site of the South brickfield. Because the land has not been developed with housing, the playing field provides a vivid impression of the conditions that prevailed in the time of Joseph and Samuel(1). The rival brickfields to the north are now laid out as Jubilee Park and a pitch and put golf course.

Contracts
In addition to his pottery and brickmaking businesses Samuel(1) diversified his interests and examples of his entrepreneurial initiatives are evident from the time of his early career. Whilst at Angel Road he supplemented the income from the pottery by hiring out the horse and cart and selling horse manure to the nursery customers[1]. In 1936 a 73 year old resident of Edmonton recalled his family in Sebastopol Road buying a pail of water for "one half-penny" from Mr. South of Water Lane (Angel Road) brought by "a horse and large barrel"[2].

Between 1907-1911 Samuel South & Sons held the contract with Tottenham Council for the removal of manure from the Council Stables[3]. An annual payment of £12[4], later raised to £15[5], was made to the Local Authority for the privilege and, presumably, the manure was carted to nurserymen and sold at a profit. The contract was lost in 1912 when a higher offer of £26 for the contract was submitted. A similar agreement was entered in 1909 when the South tender of £22 10s. [£22.50] was accepted for the right to cut and remove grass from the Lammas Lands[6] in the district[7]. It is assumed that the cut grass was to be used for animal fodder.

Another successful contract was obtained in 1909 for the supply of a variety of road materials[8]. Nine tenders were submitted to Tottenham Council including Ernest Knifton, a well known local contractor and former Snells Park neighbour of Samuel(1), and the North London Ballast & Sand Co. Ltd. The South tender to supply Rough Ballast at 5s. 0d. [25p] per yard was accepted.

Also, in 1909, the Engineer to Tottenham Council reported that there were insufficient horses for the Council's normal requirements[9] and competitive tenders were invited for the supply of horses, carts and drivers to the Authority which received the following tenders[10];

Name	Horse & Man per day	Horse, Cart & Man per day	Horse, Cart & Man per ½ day
South, S., & Sons	8s 0d	8s 6d	4s 3d
Cook, G	8s 6d	8s 6d	4s 3d
Curtis, J	8s 6d	8s 6d	4s 6d
Barker, J. H.	8s 6d	8s 6d	5s 0d
Howell, J.	8s 6d	9s 0d	5s 0d
Coston, J	8s 6d	9s 0d	5s 0d
Goddard, J	8s 6d	9s 0d	5s 0d
Lincoln, A. G	------	9s 0d	-----
Ayres, G	8s 6d	9s 0d	4s 6d
Fox, W	8s 6d	9s 0d	4s 6d
Ruggles, J	9s 0d	9s 6d	5s 0d
Bloomfield, E. T	-----	9s 0d	-----

The South tender was accepted[11]. It is interesting to note that the hire costs tendered are less than the 9s. 0d. [45p] per day that Samuel(1) was charging for the hire of a horse and cart from the Angel Road pottery some twenty years previously. The contract was renewed in 1910 and 1911 but lost the following year to a lower bidder. A similar cartage contract, primarily for refuse collection, was entered with the Wood Green Urban District Council. In 1907 Samuel(1), in competition with six other contractors, submitted the following successful tender[12]:

Item	South
Horse, Cart, Harness, and Driver for Carting Materials, &c.	8s. 6d
Horse, Harness, and Driver for Vehicles provided by Council	8s. 0d
Horse, Cart, Harness, and Driver for Watering or Flushing	8s. 6d
Horse, Van, Harness and Driver for Watering or Flushing	8s. 6d
Horse, Slop Cart, Harness, and Driver for Carting away Road Sweepings, &c.	8s. 6d
Horse, Covered Dust van, Harness, and Driver for Removing House Refuse, &c.	8s. 6d
Horse, Rotary Broom, Harness, and Driver for Sweeping Roads	8s. 6d

In the next tender year the contract was lost[13] but, displaying good business sense, South & Sons wrote to Wood Green Council *"expressing their appreciation of the courteous and businesslike treatment received by them at the hands of the officials and staff of the Council during the period of their contracts for carting, &c."*[14]. Their tender for 1909 was accepted and the contract regained[15].

By diversifying his business interests Samuel(1) could weather a down turn in one of them. For a period at the beginning of the 20th century cartage became a greater source of revenue than the pot and brickmaking activities[16].

Property and Land
Samuel(1) invested heavily in property and at the time of his death in 1919 the portfolio of houses owned by him were:[1]

Name of Road	Location	No. of Houses
Norman Avenue	Wood Green	1
Henderson Road	Edmonton	18
North Road	Edmonton	34
Mount Pleasant Road	Tottenham	6
Strode Road	Tottenham	3
St. Loys Road	Tottenham	4
Eldon Road	Wood Green	15
	Total	81

North Road and part of Henderson Road were developed on 3 acres of land, a former nursery, abutting the Edmonton brickfield that Samuel had purchased in 1902 from Jonathan Denny[2], a retired Corn Merchant of Wandsworth. Joshua Pedley and Charles May of Pedley May & Fletcher provided the mortgage enabling Samuel(1) to finance the purchase[3]. Houses on the site were erected by a speculative builder who was unable to pay for the bricks supplied by the adjacent South brickfield. The houses were accepted by Samuel(1) in settlement of the debt[4].

Properties and land in the vicinity of the White Hart Lane Potteries were also acquired. Pipers Court, some 200 yards east of the pottery, was purchased in 1909[5] and was later occupied by Samuel(1)'s son, John South. In addition to a large house the property of some 1¾ acres included a coachman's lodge and stabling for six horses together with a long run of sheds that had been used as a rope walk by a previous occupier[6]. Nearby in Devonshire Hill Lane, and close to Devonshire Hill Farm, Samuel(1) bought River House and an adjoining 35 acres of land in 1912 for the sum of £4,100[7]. Once again, Pedley and May provided a mortgage of £3,000, at a rate of 4.5%, towards the purchase price[8]. An abandoned stretch of the New River flowed through the garden and Samuel(1) bought the bed of the river separately for a further payment of £10[9]. Initially, River House was occupied by tenants but later became the home of his son, Samuel(2) and his family.

In 1915 Tottenham Council, seeking a site for an isolation hospital for the treatment of infectious diseases within the District, made an approach to Samuel(1) for the purchase of some 14½ acres of the Devonshire Hill Lane land[10]. A purchase price of £8,220 was agreed but, in the event, the Local Government Board refused to sanction the loan necessary for the Council to proceed with the sale. Again, in 1918, the Council sought to lease River House for hospital purposes. By that time, Samuel(2) was occupying the property and the plan failed to materialise for the second time.

That same year, 1915, a field of 5¾ acres, adjoining the western boundary of White Hart Lane Potteries, was acquired from the London County Council. A purchase price of £1,800 was paid together with the exchange of 4½ acres of the Devonshire Hill Lane land which Samuel(1) had bought three years earlier.

Estate
Samuel(1) had drawn up his last will in 1899 whilst living at Devonshire Hill Farm and appointed his eldest son, Samuel South(2) and Robert Buckle, who was employed as a solicitors clerk by Pedley, May & Fletcher, as executors and trustees. Robert, of White Cottage, White Hart Lane, is better known as "Bobby" Buckle, a founder member of the amateur Tottenham Hotspur, who was to remain a lifelong friend of the younger Samuel(2). He received a bequest of £50 for carrying out his duties under the will. Probate was granted to the executors on 2 July 1919 and the Estate, comprising the pottery and other interests, was valued for probate purposes at £46,057.

After leaving personal chattels to his widow Samuel(1) left detailed instructions about the disposal of the remainder of his Estate. Firstly, the trustees were empowered to conduct the pottery and brick making activities (although the brickfield was not operational at the time of Samuel's death). If, however, either of the businesses made losses for two consecutive years then they were directed to either sell or wind up the business concerned. Directions were also given for the executors and trustees to realise the residuary Estate, primarily, the property interests, although empowered to postpone such realisation as they thought fit and for the trust to receive the rental income. From the monies and property held in the trust a yearly income of £150 was to be paid to the widow and equal shares of the trust income to each of the children after attaining the age of 21.

Probate granted Samuel(2) and Robert Buckle set about realising the residuary Estate in accordance with the requirements of the will. The largest land holding was the 30 remaining acres adjacent to River House that Samuel(1) had acquired in 1912[1] and for which a probate value of £440 per acre had been agreed[2]. Seven acres were sold to three of the South brothers[3], John, Charles and Alfred with a mortgage granted by the trustees[4]. A further five acres were sold to Edward Cole[5], the owner of the pottery adjoining Souths' premises, again on a mortgage similarly granted[6], with the remainder retained by the Estate. In 1921 Tottenham Council purchased all three parcels of land for their housing scheme[7].

Smaller disposals were also made. Part of the Pipers Court land was purchased by Taylor Walker & Co. Ltd.[8], brewers, and a parcel of the River House land was sold to William Clatworthy[9], later becoming the site of the White Hart Public House. Samuel(2) and John South acquired River House[10] and Pipers Court[11] respectively, the properties they already occupied. In 1923 the executors sold the Snells Park house to the Edmonton Board of Guardians[12] for the sum of £1,075 sanctioned by the Ministry of Health[13]. The house was adapted for use as offices by the Relieving Officers of the Edmonton East, Edmonton West and North Tottenham Districts with the upper floor converted into a flat for the Edmonton Relieving Officer and rented to him at £52 per annum[14]. The Board also bought the mahogany dining table, gas fittings and linoleum floor coverings from the Estate for £7[15].

It was not until 1925 that the executors disposed of the former brickfield at Bury Street, Edmonton, to Edmonton Council who wished to acquire the land for use as playing fields[16]. Negotiations continued over several months with the Council making an initial offer of £3,860 whilst the executors sought £4,500 pointing out that probate had been agreed at £4,300. In the event, a price of £4,000 was agreed and, although not expressed, there was the possibility of a Compulsory Purchase Order being implemented had an agreement not been reached. The sale was completed in May 1925[17]and the site was developed for the Henry Barrass[18]Stadium and Sports Field.

Discretion, permitted by the will, had been exercised by the co-executors and trustees with regard to the disposal of the 81 rented houses owned by Samuel(1) at the time of his death. The ownership of the houses was assigned to the other nine children (excluding Samuel(2))[19]. Later, Alice South, Walter South, John South and Arthur South became the trustees[20]. Maintenance and administration of the houses was undertaken by South Brothers[21], a building company that was founded by Walter, Arthur and Alfred South in 1922[22]. Over the years, a number of the houses have been sold and the proceeds distributed to the beneficiaries whose descendants continue to receive a modest income from the remaining properties.

A further provision of the will stipulated that when each of Samuel(1)'s sons had attained the age of 21 (all of the sons had reached maturity by 1919) the plant, stock and effects of the pottery together with the lease of the White Hart Lane premises, were to be offered to "any one of my sons… notwithstanding he may be a trustee of this my will……. and may then be manager thereof". In the event that the offer was refused the pottery would be offered to the other sons in order of seniority and, ultimately, sold. A similar provision had also been made with respect to the brick field.

Although not named, Samuel(2) was the eldest son, the manager of the pottery and one of the two nominated trustees. He exercised the prerogative to buy the business and the arrangement reached with Estate required that he surrender any other rights that he may have under the trust. The sale price was to be determined by two independent valuers each instructed by the vendors and purchaser. The method of payment was also laid down with the purchaser making an initial payment of one third of the agreed sale price and the remainder paid at six monthly intervals over five years at 4% interest.

The independent assessment of the White Hart Lane Potteries has not survived but some attempt at a possible valuation can be made by breaking down the total probate value of the Estate. Probate values of some components are known and, after making a subjective assessment of the other items, a suggested allocation could be:

Item	Amount	Comment
Devonshire Hill Lane land (inc. River House)*	£13,200	£440 x 30 acres
Brickfield land*	£4,300	
Houses (est.)	£18,225	say £225 x 81 houses
Pipers Court (est.)	£1, 000	
West Field (potteries)	£2, 640	based on £440 per acre
43 Snells Park**	£1,075	
Total	£40,440	
Unaccounted balance (say)	£5,560	
Total Probate Value	£46,000	

*known probate value   ** known sale value

The projected balance of £5,560 would be available for personal effects, monies, investments, the pottery and other unidentified items of the Estate. With regard to the pottery, the land, with the exception of the field to the west of the site (separately identified), was leased and the potential value of the business was likely to be assessed on the plant, machinery, stock at hand and goodwill together with the value of the horses. A speculative sum of, say, £2,500/£3,500 could be proposed for the pottery. It must be cautioned, however, that in the above calculation minor variations in the value of the houses have a significant effect on the unaccounted balance.

In a separate deal[23] Samuel(2) also bought the adjoining field to the west of the pottery land that his late father had acquired from the London County Council in 1915 for future clay workings. The best estimate on the available evidence is to suggest that a sum in the region of £6,000 was involved for both transactions. Samuel(2) borrowed "against everything he had"[24] which placed a strain on his resources until the debt was repaid[25].

South Brothers[1]

After the death of Samuel South(1) in 1919 and the acquisition of the pottery from his Estate by their older brother, Samuel(2), three of the sons did not remain with the business. Walter, Arthur and Alfred left the family firm and founded South Brothers, builders, with each brother holding an equal share. Over the next twenty years some 100 houses were built, primarily in the Tottenham area. Most were sold although some properties were retained and rented out. Walter was concerned with office administration and collection of rents, Alfred dealt with finance and Arthur was a carpenter. Alfred (A. J. South) also invested in property on his own account. In addition, South Brothers administered and maintained the houses held within the family trust, South Estates. Eventually, an office was built in St. Loys Road, Tottenham, N. 17.

A small development of four pairs of semi-detached houses was built further afield at St. Michael's Road in Broxbourne, Hertfordshire, one of which one was occupied by Walter and his family from 1932[2]. He continued to drive from his home to the Tottenham office of South Brothers until the age of 79. The three bedroom houses with two reception rooms, bathroom and kitchen together with 200 ft. back garden and garage were offered for sale at £850 freehold. A mortgage over 20 years could be secured by a deposit of £54 8s. 0d. [54.40] and repayments of £1 5s. 6d. [£1.27] per week. The profit margin was small, about £50 on each house.

House building ceased on the outbreak of WW2 and post war the building firm, now joined by Eric, the son of Alfred South, initially concentrated on war damage work and, later, private contracts and maintenance of the South Estate and South Brothers rented houses. South Brothers ceased active trading in 1969 but Eric South continues to administer the remaining rented houses of South Estates, South Brothers and his father's estate.

Samuel South(2)
1853-1919

1876 - 1899

The eldest of Samuel(1) and Alice South's ten children was born on the 3 September 1876 and given his father's name. Living in Angel Road, Edmonton, the family were not far from the pottery owned by Samuel senior. Samuel(2) received an elementary education at a private school in Brettenham Road, Edmonton, for a fee of one shilling per week[1], before entering his father's business[2].

The Elementary Education Act 1876 placed a responsibility upon parents to ensure that children received an elementary education and a compulsory attendance up to the age of ten was imposed by the 1880 Education Act. Family tradition has it that Samuel(2) commenced work at his father's White Hart Lane Potteries at the age of twelve. However, the employment of minors required production of a "Certified copy of an Entry of Birth"for the purposes of the earlier Act and the certificate for Samuel(2) is dated April 1890 some 5 months before his fourteenth birthday.

The 1876 Act prohibited the employment of children between the ages of 10 and 14 unless either a certificate of proficiency in reading, writing or elementary arithmetic was obtained or there was proof of attendance at a certified school[3]. Such prohibition did not apply if the employment did not interfere with the "efficient elementary instruction" of the child[4]. There can be little doubt that Samuel(2) was working in some capacity at the pottery by the age of 12 and, probably, earlier. The Angel Road pottery was close by and his father, Samuel(1), had been in employment at a young age.

Samuel(2) was soon immersed in learning the pottery trade and working 56 hours a week acquiring the skills of a potmaker[5]. By the age of fifteen he was also stoking kilns and driving a horse and wagon delivering pots to customers[6]. Because it was primarily a cash business he also collected money due from the nurserymen[7]. Returning through lonely lanes and streets with an attractive cargo Samuel(2) equipped himself with a "Life Preserver" and horn whistle for protection and to raise the alarm in the event of a criminal attack[8]. The "Life Preserver" is a formidable weapon having a flexible shaft 8½ ins. long, possibly of whale-bone, and a lead weighted end, bound with cord. In use it was intended to be aimed at the arms or legs in order to disable the assailant. A blow to the head could easily result in fatal injuries. There is no record of the "Life Preserver" having been used in anger and it remains a serviceable weapon.

There were unpleasant tasks to perform[9]. At night Samuel(2) would be sent by his father to check the kilns and stoke the boiler in the drying shed. The stoke hole was the resort of tramps and on one occasion, apprehensive of an aggressive "visitor", he avoided a confrontation and returned home. On confessing to his father that the boiler had not been stoked, Samuel(2) was made to return and remedy the omission. He also worked at the Edmonton brickfield where an unpleasant chore of a more personal nature became necessary. A relative, who was an employee, had developed a drinking problem. In later years, Samuel(2) recalled being instructed by his father to remove bottles that had been hidden amongst the brick stacks much to his own disquiet.

A cousin, Walter Barnard, was a childhood friend, and the pair went to watch informal "trial of strength" contests between local inhabitants who gathered around the boundary area of Tottenham High Road and Edmonton Fore Street[10]. Contests might include races carrying a hod of bricks or sack of grain, pushing a barrow load of bricks or pulling a trap between the shafts[11]. Wagers were laid on the competitors and, occasionally, there was a bare knuckle fight[12]. Walter's brother, Alfred, was a prize fighter and may have participated in bouts at the "boundary"[13]. Whether Samuel(2) ever indulged in any of these activities will never be known.

Tottenham Terrace 1899 - 1908
On the 14 September 1899 Samuel(2), now aged 23, was driven from the family home at Devonshire Hill Farm to his wedding. His bride was Emily Maud King, a demonstrator at the Singer Sewing Machine shop in Tottenham High Road[1], who lived in Union Road, Edmonton. The ceremony took place at the Edmonton Congregational Church, an impressive gothic building at the southern end of Snells Park. Members of the South and King families were worshippers at the Church[2] and the bride and groom had both attended the Sunday School[3]. Emily King, aged 12, had received a bible as the prize for the highest attendance marks during 1888. A one-time teacher at the Sunday school was Edward Cole[4], owner

of the pottery adjoining the South premises in White Hart Lane. The relationship between the two families extended beyond their business rivalry.

Minister Thomas Bagley officiated and, being a nonconformist church, the local Registrar, Edwin Crusha, was also present. Many years later, at the time of his golden wedding anniversary, Samuel (2) reminisced that after he had paid the licence fee, the Registrar asked for an extra penny for the stamp needed on the certificate[5]. Having no change, Samuel(2), said *"Can I owe it you?"*. Apparently the debt was never paid and became a standing joke between the two men.

The bride and groom had been conveyed in an open, horse-drawn, carriage driven by William "Billy" Mudge[6] who became a life-long friend of Samuel(2). "Billy" Mudge was a well known Tottenham character operating a cartage business and, later, a car hire service. His services may have been required again nine days later for another family wedding when Samuel(2)'s cousin, Florence South, daughter of Joseph South junior, married at the same church on 23 September 1899.

Home for the newly married couple was 2 Tottenham Terrace, one of a terrace of 12 three storey dwellings located on the northern loop of White Hart Lane a few yards from the High Road. It was here that the first three of their eight children were born, Elsie b. 1900, Hilda b. 1902, and Gladys b. 1906. With a growing family, washing was sent to Alice Asser who lived nearby in Cottage Terrace[7]. A short distance to the west stood two grand properties, Trafalgar House and Arlington House, both of which had large ornamental gardens.

Trafalgar House had been formerly occupied by Dr. William Robinson (1777-1848), the noted historian of Tottenham, Edmonton and Enfield. It is rumoured that his father, also William (1737-1808), had an affair with Ann Nelson (1760-1783), the sister of Horatio, Lord Nelson, and that a son, William junior, resulted from the relationship[8]. Hence the name given to the house. At the time Samuel(2) moved to Tottenham Terrace, Trafalgar House was the home of Joshua Pedley, senior partner of Pedley, May & Fletcher, the Souths' solicitors. Samuel(2) was a friend of one of the two Welfare brothers[9], gardeners at Trafalgar House, and who had been a guest at his wedding[10]. The South children were sometimes allowed to visit the garden[11] and collect Mulberry leaves to feed the silk worms kept by them[12].

Another life long friendship was made with Robert "Bobby" Buckle, a founder member and secretary of the amateur Tottenham Hotspur Football Club. Bobby was a Solicitor's Clerk with Pedley, May & Fletcher and was an executor under the will of the older Samuel. Samuel(2) was a keen supporter of Spurs throughout his life, buying a £1 share (no. 1649) in the professional club in 1903[13].

Snells Park 1908 - 1917

In 1908[14] the family moved from Tottenham Terrace to 39 Snells Park, Edmonton, which was one house away from Samuel(1) and close to the Congregational Church where Samuel(2) and Maud had been married nine years before. No. 39, was a semi-detached villa style house, having nine rooms, on three floors[15] with a half stucco front elevation and decorative mouldings over the sash window openings[16]. There was a side tradesmen's entrance with a nearby chute to the coal cellar beneath[17]. A maid was employed complete with white cap and apron. One of the maids "Winnie" Brown, was married to a South employee who delivered milk to Snells Park provided by cows kept in the leased fields next to the South pottery.

The South children went to St James Church of England School in Grove Road at the northern end of Snells Park[18] where the alphabet was learnt by copying letters on the blackboard into a tray of fine sand. Pocket money was spent in the sweet shop opposite the school. The shop parades either side of busy Edmonton Fore Street and Tottenham High Road were only a short walk away. Horse and carts delivering milk and meat plied the local streets and large horse drawn drays from the two Tottenham brewers, Whitbread and Fremlins, supplied barrels of beer to the local hostelries. The butcher who delivered to the Snells Park household walked the horse through his shop, past the meat on display, to and from the stable at the rear.

Memories of the South family have recalled an "almost a kind of village life"[19] with a "mixed population"[20]. The immediate neighbours were the Davies family, whose children played with the young Souths, and the Atkins[21], who ran a laundry from a building in their garden. Others in the vicinity were Hatch (councillor)[9], Harrison (builder's merchant), Cartwright (solicitor) and Barton (proprietor of "Dicky Bird's" confectioners). Opposite, at 46 Snells Park, Mr. Lawman, the local Relieving Officer lived in a similar semi-detached house. In 1911 the family of a young Edith Fisk (later Knight) rented No 46 Snells Park and soon became friends with the South children. Edith's family were local printers and her uncle, Fred Fisk, was a local bookseller and local historian.

Sunday services were well attended at the Congregational Chapel[10] and the South children sat with their grandmother King in the gallery[11]. Anne King lived close by and it was the task of one of the children to take her a roast Sunday lunch[12]. Sunday school was held in a hall off Fore Street which had a library and a youth club[13]. Outings were arranged to Chingford woods. A local resident recalls a member of the South family singing solos with the choir[14]. One member of the choir, May Blyth, later achieved renown at Covent Garden opera house[15]. A fund was organised at the chapel by the father of Edith Knight in order to allow May to receive voice training[16]. Later, she married a noted conductor, Aylmer Buestt, in some pomp at the Congregational Chapel[17].

During the 1914-1918 war, wardens patrolled the district and families placed a card in the window bearing the letter "P" overnight if they wanted to be awakened in the event of an possible air raid[18]. Memories have been recalled of Zeppelin airships passing overhead on bombing missions and, later in the war, German aircraft[19].

The family continued to grow with the births of Samuel(3) b. 1909, Charles b. 1910, James (Jim) b. 1912 and Edwin (Ted) b. 1915. After nine years at Snells Park another move was made.

River House 1917 - 1926
Samuel South(1) had bought River House in Devonshire Hill Lane, Tottenham, in 1912. River House, so called because an abandoned section of the New River ran through the garden, was about a quarter mile from the White Hart Lane Potteries. The house had been rented to Alexander Field and his family but in 1917 Samuel(2) moved in. His eighth, and last, child Joyce was born at River House the following year.

Surrounded by fields, the house was reached by a narrow, winding, unlit lane leading from White Hart Lane near Rectory Farm. No other houses were passed on the half mile walk to River House and the nearest neighbours lived at Devonshire Hill Farm some 120 yards west of the house at the termination of the lane. Wide strips of manorial waste land lay either side of the lane between River House and the farm. In 1921, Samuel(2) sought to purchase the waste land of some third of an acre for £191[1]. The agents of the Lord of the Manor were prepared to accept the offer but Tottenham Council, which had an interest in the land, were not so disposed and the transaction was not completed[2].

Situated on the crest of a hill, the front (southern) elevation of River House gave a panoramic view over north London with the dome of St. Pauls Cathedral visible on clear days[3]. However, it was the rear (northern) aspect which gave direct access on to Devonshire Hill Lane and used as the usual entrance by the family[4]. Opposite River House a stile gave access to open fields extending to Weir Hall in Edmonton[5]. On Sundays, an enterprising workman from the South pottery set up a stall by the stile and sold refreshments to Tottenham inhabitants taking the opportunity for a pleasant stroll in the rural environment[6]. Refreshments and sweets were also available from the Devonshire Hill farmhouse[7]. On occasion, in an attempt to emulate these entrepreneurs, the South children, without their parent's knowledge, tried to sell apples from the orchard in the River House garden[8].

A rambling L-shaped building, River House comprised two, formerly separate, sections with an older cottage comprising the west wing[9]. At an unknown date, the two properties had been connected by a construction known to the South family as the "Stone Passage"[10]. A house, yard and garden together a barn on the site of the older cottage, is recorded in the 1798 Wyburd survey of Tottenham commissioned by Henry Sperling. Forty years later, on the 1844 Tithe map, the connected dwellings creating River House are shown. The cottage was very damp and had been constructed in a rudimentary fashion, there were no footings and the baked clay floor slabs had been laid on a thin layer of ash[11]. Roof timbers consisted of split tree trunks with the bark attached[12]. A possible explanation for the poor construction is that the cottage was converted from the existing outbuilding shown on the 1798 survey map.

Accommodation in the cottage section of River House comprised two bedooms on the upper floor. Downstairs there was a scullery and kitchen with a large bread oven, iron kitchen range[13], walk-in larder with slate shelves, an ice chest and a musket rack over the fireplace[14]. A well was situated in the courtyard[15] and, although filled in later, a garden footpath constructed over the site continued to subside up to the 1950s[16]. The kitchen gave access to the Stone Passage with a door into the courtyard which served as the usual entrance[17]. Stairs from the passage descended to the cellar which extended under the area of the main house. Poultry and game were hung in the cellar and a wine bin was used to store jellies, blancmanges, and eggs pickled in Isinglass[18]. The cellar was prone to flooding and on those occasions the accumulated water was pumped out[19].

A further doorway from the Stone Passage opened onto a passage into the main section of the house with two large living rooms and a serving pantry adjoining the dining room[20]. Upstairs there were five bedrooms, three rooms of which interconnected, in addition to the rooms in the older wing. A solitary bathroom served the needs of the large family. Sanitary arrangements were supplemented, in the early years, by an outside privy with a double seat.

The large garden had a frontage of some 500 ft. to Devonshire Hill Lane extending from the later site of the White Hart Public House westwards to the footpath that connected the lane with White Hart Lane. Rose beds were laid out nearest to the house with a vegetable garden beyond[21]. A timber bridge provided a crossing over the section of the New River that cut through the grounds[22]. To the south stood three mature chestnut trees and a large lawn from which a gate opened onto a field leading to Pipers Court at the foot of the hill where John South, Samuel(2)'s brother, and his family lived[23]. It was a well used route when the children visited Pipers Court to play with their cousins[24]. Land to the east of the house had been planted as an orchard[25] and was the target for "scrumping" apples by boys from the newly developed Tottenham Council housing estate[26]. One of the culprits later became an employee at the pottery[27].

River House was in a neglected condition and refurbishment was in progress as the South family moved in[28]. Living rooms were decorated with dark patterned wallpaper, floral designs in the bedrooms and wood-grained varnished paper on the kitchen walls[29]. Because of the flock wallpaper, the drawing room was known as the " Red Room " [30]. The garden was considerably overgrown and gradually restored[31]. Although abandoned in 1852 by the construction of the Wood Green tunnel, the section of the New River running through the garden remained in water but over the coming years was filled in with spoil brought from the pottery[32]. In addition to the New River there were several ponds in the area and it was a frequent occur-rence for passing children who had fallen in to be brought to River House for " drying out"[33]. Three rather fierce geese on one of the ponds in the lane were later taken to the pottery[34].

River House garden was an ideal playground for the younger South children although not always to their mutual enjoyment[35]. During one particularly robust game of "Cowboys and Indians" with her elder brothers, Jim and Ted, Joyce was put in a large drainpipe the large garden and left. Some time later, her disappearance was only discovered by her mother when she failed to return to the house for her tea. In later years, Joyce, the youngest of the eight children, would complain that she was always the Indian!

Joe Dew, a long serving employee at the pottery (he had been a guest at Samuel(2)'s wedding) became the gardener at River House along with another pottery workman, Teddy Brinkley[36]. Both men jealously guarded their domain and the South children were careful not to encroach onto the vegetable garden[37]. Even their mother was sometimes intimidated and waited until the gardeners had left for the day before picking the crop[38]. Later, an ex-policeman took over as gardener but left because of some unrecorded misconduct in the kitchen garden with one of the maids[39].

There was domestic help in the house, with one and sometimes two, live-in maids who came from a Salvation Army establishment in Hackney[40]which cared for girls who had suffered deprivation, including abuse, at home[41]. South relatives regularly visited River House on Sundays[42]and it was usual for up to fifteen people to sit down for lunch. In a demonstration of his sense of fair play and recognising that the maids would be busy clearing away and washing up after the meal, Samuel(2) would carve the first (and the best!) slices of meat from the joint for them much to the annoyance of his waiting family[43].

Although the domestic assistance suggests a privileged upbringing, nevertheless, the South children were not spoilt and were subject to the firm discipline of their parents, particularly their mother, Maud, who had methods of making her opinion known[44]. On one occasion[45], she became exasperated at the regular lateness of Samuel(2) and his elder sons returning from the pottery for their evening meal. They arrived home one evening to find that a meal had not been prepared and Maud South sitting at the un-laid dining table, apparently, reading a book (which she later admitted was upside down). Her protest had been well made and the men became more punctual.

Anne King, now a widow, came to live with her daughter and son-in-law at River House having a bed-sitting room above the kitchen in the older wing where she helped with repairing and darning the children's clothes[46]. She dressed in a Victorian manner wearing dark dresses with high necks, long sleeves and long skirts and attended chapel each Sunday wearing a bonnet[47]. Anne died, aged 83, in 1920 and the South children were taken to her room to say their farewells[48].

A routine that spanned the years at River House was established at Christmas[49]. Samuel(2) would visit Covent Garden and return laden with boxes of apples, oranges, grapes and, sometimes, pineapples. Another trip was made into the country where several turkeys were bought direct from the farmer and brought back to River House unplucked, undrawn and with heads still attached. The poultry and fruit was distributed amongst his family, business friends and retired, long serving, pottery employees. After the Second World War the tradition was continued on a smaller scale. The author recalls helping to carry the birds, by their necks, into New River House where they were placed on sheets covering the furniture in the drawing room.

River House 1926 - 1936
By 1925 the housing estate developed by Tottenham Council, on the land sold to them by the executors of Samuel(1)[1] and others[2], extended to the

southern boundary of River House. An agreement was reached which allowed the Local Authority to construct a sewer across part of the River House land enabling Samuel(2) to contemplate development of his own property[3]. In 1926 he submitted three planning applications; to extend River House; to erect fifteen houses on the land to the west of the house extending to the footpath; and to build four houses on the garden to the east of River House. The proposed dwellings were to connect to the Council drainage system but, although planning permission was granted, not all of the plans proceeded.

The project to build to the east of River House was abandoned and, in September 1927, Whitbread & Co. Ltd bought the land from Samuel(2)[4]. Together with adjoining land, previously sold by the executors of Samuel(1)[5], the White Hart Public House was built on the combined site. Samuel(2) attended the official opening of the White Hart on December 12, 1928[6]. There were also amendments to the plan for the western development, and, in the event, a terrace of six houses was built for Samuel(2) by South Brothers. Known as River Terrace, two of the houses were occupied by his married daughters, Elsie and Gladys, a third sold and the remaining three properties rented to tenants. The houses were later incorporated as 141-151 Devonshire Hill Lane when the road was developed and re-numbered. The remaining land, between the end of the terrace and the Ash Path, and now isolated from River House, continued to be cultivated as a vegetable garden although the crops were sometimes stolen by passers-by[7]. Within a few years, this land was sold and a further terrace of eight houses was erected by D. Pettit & Son in 1934[8].

The alterations to River House went ahead as originally proposed. The older west wing was demolished and a two storey extension added to the eastern end of the existing house. The extension added a cloakroom, large kitchen and scullery to the ground floor with three bedrooms upstairs. Gas continued to supply the lighting for River House but the lamps suspended from the ceilings in the additional rooms could be controlled by a wall mounted valve[9]. Further permission was obtained to erect a garage to the front of River House[10]. There was accommodation for two cars with an outside car wash area. The interior was timber clad with fitted storage cupboards and radiators that were heated by an external coal stove.

Although able to drive Samuel(2) did not believe that a successful business and safe driving could be conducted simultaneously. A series of chauffeurs were employed. His cars included a Belsize[11], a Siddely-Deasey[12]and finally, from the mid 1930s, an Armstrong Siddeley "Long 20" which will be remembered by many of his grandchildren who were taken for a ride in the car as a "treat". It was an impressive vehicle with a sliding glass partition dividing the driver from the rear compartment which included two folding occasional seats and a drop-leaf table. Passengers enjoyed the comfort of upholstered cloth seats and deep pile carpeting. The exterior boasted deep running boards, powerful twin horns and the familiar Sphinx mascot on the bonnet. The Armstrong Siddeley sales brochure for 1933 lists an ex-works cost of £725 for the "Long 20" model[13].

Like his father, Samuel(2) continued to maintain close contact with his nurserymen customers. One of them, Charles Pratley whose nursery in Bury Street, Edmonton, was not far from the former South brickfield, became a friend. It is believed that the nurseryman assisted Samuel(2) financially, perhaps with the purchase of the pottery from the estate of Samuel South(1)[14]. On the death of Charles Prately in 1929 Samuel(2) was appointed an executor and was active in the settlement of the estate[15]. He performed a similar function in 1931 for the estate of John Corrie, a well known local cartage contractor[16].

Samuel(2) was a staunch supporter of The National Association of Horticultural Pottery Manufacturers which represented the interests of the flower pot makers. The Association had about 30 members including the neighbouring pottery of E. G Cole & Sons and the larger potters, Sankey of Bulwell, Nottingham, and Ward of Darleston, Midlands[17]. Regular meetings were held at the Hotel Russell, Russell Square, London, W.C. 1 with annual conferences at seaside venues such as Torquay, Eastbourne or Cromer which Samuel(2) regularly attended often accompanied in the Armstrong car by the Secretary, Frank Forney. Frank Forney was active in local politics and had been introduced to the Association by a fellow Councillor, Sidney Cole. He retired from the post because of ill health and during the 1963/64 Conference in Eastbourne, and at the instigation of the Ward representatives, a firm of Midlands accountants was appointed to take over the Secretarial duties. By that time a number of the smaller potteries had closed and it can not have been long afterwards that the Association was wound up. The whereabouts of the records of the Association have not been located. Samuel(2) also became a keen member of the Wood Green Rotary Club, an association of local business men, and attended their annual conferences.

Unlike his rival potmaker, Sidney Cole of E. G. Cole & Son who was a member of the Wood Green Council serving as Mayor and Alderman, Samuel(2) did not enter public life. He was, however, well known and respected in the local community to the extent that his visits to Southwold, his regular holiday haunt, were noted in the weekly local paper[18].

River House 1936-1956
One by one the older South children married and left home, Elsie (1926), Hilda (1928), Gladys, (1928), Charles (1933) and Samuel(3) (1934). By the time Jim South married in 1936 only Ted and Joyce remained living with their parents. River House was too large for the remaining family and, in any event, was in need of modernisation[1]. It was cold and draughty and continued to be lit by gas. Maud South would have preferred to move away and houses were viewed in Southgate and Enfield. Samuel(2), however, refused to consider a move which was not within walking distance of the pottery and family objections were overruled[2].

In 1936 and 1937 plans were submitted to Tottenham Council for the erection of a new house to the west of the existing River House. It was proposed to demolish the existing house and construct a terrace of three houses on the site. The 1927 River House extension was incorporated within the terrace and survives as 133 Devonshire Hill Lane. The new house, which stands today, was named New River House with the postal address of 139 Devonshire Hill Lane N. 17.

Samuel(2) had a strong sense of family and three of his sons Samuel(3), Charles and Ted had joined him at the family pottery. Jim, however, was reluctant to do so but strengthened the horticultural connection by going to work at the nursery of William Cull[3]. Later, he moved to the Millfield Nursery of Henry May and, in 1936, with the assistance of his father, went on to acquire Oak Nursery at Goffs Oak in Hertfordshire[4]. The nursery was sold in 1952[5]. His daughter, Hilda, had married Cyril Beech, who, in 1938, founded Resistances Ltd., a company which manufactured and supplied resistors to the electrical industry[6]. Cyril died, aged 42, in 1940 and Hilda replaced him as Managing Director. Samuel (2) was appointed a director and provided financial support to the company. The company traded from premises in Finsbury Park until 1967 when it was sold to Alma Components Ltd. of Diss, Norfolk.

Samuel(2) became president of the Wood Green Rotary Club in 1936 and quotations from his speeches made during the presidential year, and reported in the local press, express both his personal and business philosophies:

"Anyone can throw bricks and pull things down but not everyone can build up"[7]

"We are all so inclined to become immersed in business and trades that we are liable to lose sight of what is required of us citizens"[8].

Large industrial groupings were *"without a soul to be damned or a body to be kicked"*[9].

In addition to the more formal charity works of the Rotary Club, Samuel(2) was always ready to offer practical advice and material help in an unassuming way to local organisations such as the Boy Scouts. Regular donations were made to the Salvation Army and the London City Mission. The employment of the girls from the Salvation Army Home was a way of assisting those who came from deprived backgrounds. For many years a Roman Catholic nun would visit Maud South to collect donations for her order. In the late 1940s, the author, whilst a pupil at Devonshire Hill Primary school, recalls being summoned by the headmaster who requested that he ask his grandfather if the school could buy "seconds" from the pottery. The message was duly conveyed to Samuel(2) who gruffly replied *"Souths don't sell seconds!"* A few days later a South lorry was delivering flower pots to the school for which, of course, no charge had been made.

One of the pleasures of Samuel(2) was touring with friends in the Armstrong Siddeley. In the summer of 1939, driven by Charles Tompkins, he toured Scotland accompanied by J. H. "Jimmy" Martin, builders merchant of West Green, Tottenham, and Arthur Tuck of the G & A Tuck pottery, Waltham Abbey[10]. The party reached John O' Groats[11] but war was declared on 3 September 1939 and the party returned early[12]. Three of his sons enlisted and served overseas, Samuel(3) in Burma and Charles in Italy. The youngest son Ted, a sapper in the Royal Engineers, received fatal wounds during the Dunkirk retreat when enemy aircraft strafed the village of Les Moires in May 1940. His family, who had never seen him in uniform, did not receive news of his fate until March 1941. Ted left a widow having married in July 1939.

Preparations for war had been made at New River House. A brick built air raid shelter was constructed in the garden. Each of the thick walls incorporated a section of brickwork built with a sand and cement mortar which could be knocked out for an escape route if the entrance became obstructed. During air raid warnings, Gladys, who was living at 145 Devonshire Hill Lane and her family came to sleep on the bunk beds in the shelter. At the time of the London blitz, Gladys and her sister, Joyce, wrote a list of the dates and times of each raid on the wall and which remained visible for many years thereafter. As the air raids continued Samuel(2) gradually stopped coming to the shelter preferring to stay in the house although sleeping down stairs rather than his bedroom on the first floor. New River House was made the collection point for a neighbourhood stirrup pump which could be used to extinguish minor fires caused by incendiary bombs. A large water storage tank was installed near the front gate and the front wall bore the stencilled notice " Stirrup pump here".

During an air raid on the night of 30 October 1940 a high explosive bomb fell in the back garden of 133 Devonshire Hill Lane, the former 1927 extension to River House, and not far from the South shelter[13]. The bomb did not detonate. Although a bomb disposal squad attended, the family always maintained that the unit had been unable to expose and defuse the bomb, which, presumably remains active today somewhere underground.

After the war, Samuel(2) set about putting his affairs in order. A last will was made leaving his Estate in trust to provide an income for his widow together with directions for the distribution of the Estate on her death. In 1949 he bought a burial plot in Edmonton cemetery for himself and Maud close to the resting place of his father[14]. Although control of the pottery had been effectively transferred to his sons, Samuel(3) and Charles, by the creation of a limited company, nevertheless, Samuel(2) continued to play an active part and would visit the pottery daily, including week-ends, up to his last illness. On occasion, when a car was not available for him, Samuel(2) collected money for the weekly wage roll at the pottery from Barclays Bank in Tottenham High Road travelling by bus and carrying the cash on him much to the consternation of his wife.

On 14 September 1949 Samuel(2) and Maud celebrated the 50th anniversary of their marriage. Over 100 guests attended a golden wedding celebration at the St. Benet Fink's church hall, Lordship Lane, including their three surviving sons, four daughters and seventeen grandchildren. The anniversary was reported in the local press and Samuel(2) was variously described as the "Flower-Pot King" and "The man who makes millions"[9]. An interview with him was included :-

"Work has been Mr. South's main interest in his life, though for 60 years he has been a keen follower of the 'Spurs.

'They've always had good players' he opines, *'But as Arthur Rower [Manager] says it's the goals that count. Personally I don't mind what division they play in, as long as we see good football at Tottenham.'*

Hale and vigorous with a kindly twinkle in his eyes, and a robust antipathy for all *'these darn restrictions'* which are *'the bane of a businessman's life,'* Mr. South has a sovereign remedy to all who seek a full and happy life. He recommends – an honest day's work."

Aware of their father's robust views, his children arranged for posters to be displayed in the church hall admonishing "No Business! No Politics! No Strikes!"

As reported in the newspaper, Samuel(2) continued to support the Spurs football team. When home matches were played his life long friend Billy Mudge would send a car to collect him. A plated Saturday lunch would be taken to Billy. Before he left for the match, the two friends would talk and reminisce whilst Samuel(2) helped to collect the money from the fans who paid to leave their bicycles in the yard of the Mudge garage. Occasionally, much to his amusement, Samuel(1) received a tip from one of the cyclists.

Even when Samuel(2) was away a driver would continue to call for the Saturday lunch.

There were the attendance sat the weekly local Rotary lunches and at the annual conferences of The National Association of Horticultural Pottery Manufacturers. In 1952 the event was held in Eastbourne and Samuel(2) was accompanied by his eldest son Samuel(3) together with his grandsons Graham and Peter South who were now working at the White Hart Lane pottery[16]. It was with great pride that he heard the chairman announce that three generations of the South family were present.

Four years later, on Saturday 16 June 1956, Samuel(2) passed away at the Wood Green & Southgate Cottage Hospital after a short illness and three months from his eightieth birthday. He had been taken ill over the previous weekend but felt well enough to take his usual Sunday morning walk to the pottery. His condition deteriorated and he was admitted to Wood Green Cottage Hospital the following day suffering from a perforated ulcer. He suffered a series of strokes and did not recover.

The funeral took place on Thursday 21 June 1956 arranged by W Nodes Ltd., Wood Green. The cortege assembled outside New River House. Three Daimler hearses carried over 130 wreathes and floral tributes which had been received together with ten Rolls Royce limousines for the official mourners. His widow Maud was conveyed in the Armstrong Siddeley that Samuel had bought some twenty years before and in which they had enjoyed many journeys together. She was accompanied by her three surviving sons Samuel(3), Charles and James ("Jim"). Charles Tompkins, a long serving employee, was the driver.

The cortege travelled east along Devonshire Hill Lane passing the White Hart Public House that stood on the site of the orchard of the former family home (River House) and, turning left into Devonshire Road, entered White Hart Lane opposite Pipers Court. Employees of E.G .Cole & Son, the rival pottery, stood in tribute outside their premises as the procession passed. The hearse bearing the coffin paused in front of the entrance to Samuel South & Sons that had closed for the day of the funeral. Samuel(2) had made his last journey to White Hart Lane Potteries where he had worked for so long.

Proceeding via Perth Road and Lordship Lane the cortege arrived at St Benet Fink Church. The service was conducted by the Prebendary Dean of Tottenham, the Reverend C F Waton. Roland Read, president of the Wood Green Rotary Club, addressed the congregation:

I am indeed grateful for the opportunity afforded me as President of the Rotary Club of Wood Green to voice a sincere tribute to our very dear and respected member Sam. There are many of his fellow Rotarians present at this Service and it is my privilege to express on their behalf, our pride at having had Sam amongst us for over twenty eight years. He was selected President as long ago as 1936 and has been an active member ever since........We looked upon Sam as a real old English Gentleman (a character one does not often meet) and his sound advice was always welcomed and appreciated in the club. A Rotarian should aim at high ethical standards, regular attendance, a ready acquiescence when called upon to take a job, always big hearted, broad minded, thinking fairly and acting justly. Sam, had all these qualities which were evident to all who knew him, and his interpretation of these Standards will for ever remain outstanding example to us all. ....Sam always lived up to our motto "Service before Self".

After the service, the cortege made its way onto the Great Cambridge Road (A 10) and travelled north, with a police escort, to Edmonton Cemetery for the committal. The traffic lights at the junction with White Hart Lane changed to red as the hearses passed through and Samuel(3) instructed Charles Tompkins to follow them against the light. The remainder of the procession of cars followed this example.

The funeral was an impressive and a fitting tribute to a man who had contributed significantly to local business life and the community. The spread of his interests and the regard in which he was held was exemplified by the floral tributes and letters of condolence that were received from a wide circle of friends, business acquaintances and local organisations. His widow Maud survived for a further ten years with failing health and was cared for by her daughter Joyce who had remained at New River House after her marriage in 1940. Maud South died on 4 September 1966 and was interred with her husband in Edmonton Cemetery.

The life of Samuel South(2) spanned eight decades, the reign of six monarchs, from Victoria to Elizabeth II, twenty six governments of varying political complexion, fifteen prime ministers, from Disraeli to Eden, and encompassed two world wars. The period witnessed dramatic scientific and technological advances including electric light, the internal combustion engine, powered flight, moving pictures, radio and television. A year after his death the space age was born with the launch of the Russian 'Sputnik'.

Throughout his life, Samuel(2) had lived and worked within a radius of three miles and, although receiving an elementary education only, his knowledge of the wider world was increased by extensive reading particularly of non-fiction and biography. The remarks in the speeches made during his year as President of the Wood Green Rotary Club exemplified his philosophy of life and, perhaps, Samuel(2) is best summed up in the words of his son, Jim South, "……..he had a fine sense of what was right in the matter of our behaviour to one another".

Devonshire Hill Farm

After the death of his father in 1919 Samuel South(2) had taken over the lease of Devonshire Hill Farm owned by the New River Company. The farmhouse lay to the north of the White Hart Lane pottery and the farmland extended westwards over 48 acres to Wolves Lane.

The farmhouse and cottage (Ivy Cottage) were rented out and the land was used for pasture and hay fields which provided fodder for the pottery horses. Itinerant gangs of workmen were employed at haymaking [1]. A price was agreed with the "Captain" (foreman) and the teams of men would advance across the fields in formation cutting the hay with their scythes [2]. They would lunch on beer and potatoes in the field [3]. Local Scout groups held their camps in the fields and the South children also spent "nights under canvas" at the farm[4].

During WW1, in furtherance of the war effort, Government directions had been received to grow potato crops on one of the leased fields [5]. A visiting official insisted that the field was ploughed but Samuel(2) demurred knowing the condition of the clay soil. Ignoring his advice, a Ministry contractor was instructed to carry out the work and the steam plough sank into the ground up to its axles. The equipment could not be recovered until the weather had improved and Samuel(2) was vindicated. There is evidence that potatoes continued to be grown after the war because some of the entries in his bank pass books for 1920-1927 have been annotated by him and refer to monies deposited for "potatoes", "rent", "hay" and "grazing". The farm also felt the effect of the Irish "troubles" of the 1920s when a hayrick at the farm was set on fire by supporters of the I.R.A[6].

As the dependency on horses lessened with the introduction of motor transport, some thirty acres of the farm land, between the pottery and Wolves Lane, was rented out to sports clubs[7]. A refreshment pavilion was erected and lettings etc. were administered by Hilda, his daughter[8]. Amongst the teams renting the cricket, hockey and football pitches was Wood Green Town Football Club which had acquired a lease in the 1921 season and had erected a stand and tea bar for their own use[9]. In addition there was a considerable number of tennis clubs some of which also erected their own accommodation.

A few years later the New River Company embarked on a policy of disposing of their Devonshire Farm holding. Wood Green District Council purchased the sports field land in February 1930[10]and gave notice that the tenancy of Samuel(2) would expire on 29 September 1931[11]. Thirty-four of the sports clubs[12]formed the South Field's Committee"[13]to liaise with the local authority concerning their continued occupation of the playing field. The extent to which the field had been developed for sports purposes under the South occupation was demonstrated in a report by the Clerk to the Council[14]:

"....that 40 clubs were communicated with regarding renewals of tenancies. Twenty-eight clubs representing 70 courts, had renewed their tenancies; 12 clubs representing 23 courts had decided not to renew, and a provisional tenancy had been granted to one club for one court."

Prior to expiry of the lease granted to Samuel(2) the Council entered negotiations to purchase the main pavilion and groundsman's shed from him and the sale was agreed at £350[15]. The income that he had derived from the rental of the sports field is not known but some indication may be given by a report in the minutes of the Wood Green Council when the local authority agreed to the lease of a pitch, together with use of the main refreshment pavilion as a changing room, to the exotically named Indiana Ladies' Hockey Club for £30 per season[16].

Earlier, in 1928, Samuel(2) had purchased 22 acres of the formerly leased Devonshire Farm land from the New River Company for £9,000[17]. The transaction included, however, a small parcel which had been let directly by them to the Wood Green District Council for use as allotments[18]. Under the terms of the contract, the lease could only be terminated in the event that the land was required for building purposes[19]. Samuel(2) was approached by the local authority to ascertain whether he was prepared to issue a new lease for a period of 10 years[20]. He refused explaining that he had bought the land as "clay reserve" but the Council, nevertheless, had security of tenure under the existing arrangement[21].

The continuing existence of the allotments was terminated in 1935 when the parcel of land was included within 12 acres of the former New River Company land that Samuel(2) sold to the Totteridge Lane Freehold Land Company[22] at a price of £875 per acre[23]. After completion of the sale, the developers demolished the farmhouse, extended Devonshire Hill Lane westwards and built private housing. In order to accommodate the allotments, Samuel(2) agreed to lease the Council five acres of the New River land retained by him, lying to the north of the pottery, at a yearly rental of £8 per acre subject to the proviso that removal of "the top spit or the turf" was not permitted and it should be "dug up and turned in"[24]. A further 3½ acres of land to the east of the farmhouse was sold by him to Lawes & Son Ltd. in 1934 for housing development[25].

Southwold[1]
No re-telling of the life of Samuel(2) would be complete without a mention of Southwold, the small seaside town on the Suffolk coast, that he 'discovered' on a touring holiday with his wife after an illness in the early 1920's. It was the start of an association that was to last for the next 30 years. Annual holidays, with the younger South children, Jim, Ted and Joyce, were taken during the month of August.

The family "boarded" at a house, and, providing the money for provisions and the like, they would be looked after by the landlady. At first they lodged at 'Little Winks' 9 North Parade, on the sea front but later stayed at a house in Stradbroke Road near the lighthouse. A beach hut would be hired and the days spent on the shore, walking to the harbour, taking the chain ferry to Walberswick for a penny, and returning across the common.

An entertainment for the children was to watch the guests at the Grand Hotel (long since demolished) promenading in evening dress before dinner.

The older, married, South children and other members of the family would make visits. His brother, Charles, was accustomed to spending his holidays further along the coast at Lowestoft and Gorleston and would make trips to Southwold. In 1932 the two brothers travelled to north Norfolk in order to hear the last sermon of the vicar of Stiffkey, Harold Davidson[2]. The priest was unfrocked after consorting with ladies of easy virtue in London whom he claimed to be "saving" from their way of life. He was mauled by a lion whilst appearing in a side-show at Skegness in 1937 and received fatal injuries.

Here in Southwold Samuel(2), once again, made lasting friendships. Alfred Baggot, local butcher of Victoria Street, who became Mayor of the town, later wrote " I have a good many friends but ….. Sam was the first"[3]. Samuel(2) became well known in the town to the extent that Alfred Baggot suggested that he stand for Mayor of Southwold. Public life, however, was not for Samuel(2) and the offer was declined. It was whilst staying at Southwold in June 1938 that he suffered a "sudden and serious illness"[4] and underwent surgery at a Lowestoft hospital[5]. There were several weeks of convalescence before he was able to resume an active business life. During this time Samuel(2) compiled a scrapbook of newspaper cuttings and photographs which has supplied some of the information upon which this narrative is based.

After all of the children had grown up Samuel(2) and Maud continued to visit Southwold as guests at the Crown Hotel in the High Street. In their later years they would visit in the spring, summer and autumn for two or three weeks at a time. As a treat, grandchildren often travelled in the Armstrong Siddeley on the trips to either take or collect their grandparents. The author recalls accompanying them on one particular journey to Southwold. Passing through a village on the way, a man was spotted lying in a ditch by the roadside underneath a bicycle. Samuel(2) told Charles Tompkins, his driver, to stop so that assistance could be given to an apparent accident victim. The assumption was not correct. At 11 a.m. on a Good Friday morning, the "accident victim" was drunk. His address was ascertained from a passer-by and a stately procession proceeded through the village. Lead by Samuel(2) supporting the inebriate with regular exhortations to *"come on, you silly old fool"*, the author followed wheeling the bicycle and, finally, the Armstrong, travelling at a funereal pace, brought up the rear. On arrival at the house, a rather embarrassed wife opened the door and took control of her husband and his bicycle.

On the death of Samuel(2) in 1956, his friend, Alfred Baggot, arranged the signal honour for the flag to be flown at half mast on the Sailors' Reading Room, a Southwold landmark[6]. Many letters of condolence were received from local business men and other residents of the town. Since that time, Southwold has retained its charm and resisted adverse development. Samuel(2) would have little difficulty in recognising the familiar haunts of his 'second home'.

Joseph South 1822-1906

Samuel South(1) 1853-1919

Samuel South(2) 1876-1956

Samuel South(3) 1909-1968

River House (north elevation) circa 1925

Samuel South(2) in garden of River House circa 1925
Joe Dew (gardener) left - River House (south elevation) background

Entrance to White Hart Lane Potteries 1960
Pottery office opposite entrance and canteen (left)

Pierce Arrow lorry outside pottery office circa 1925

Samuel South & Sons workforce circa 1895
Samuel South(2) fourth right (in bowler hat)

A VIEW OF ONE OF THE SHEDS WHERE THE POTS ARE MADE

ONE OF
THE . .
LARGEST
MAKERS
OF
HORTICULTURAL
POTTERY
IN
ENGLAND

FROM S. SOUTH & SONS, Tottenham Potteries,
WHITE HART LANE, LONDON, N.
TELEPHONE No. 54 TOTTENHAM

Post card of potmaking shed circa 1925 (with overprint)

Clay mill 1927

Leo Warner (wheelwright) left
Bill Cox (blacksmith)

Claypit 1960

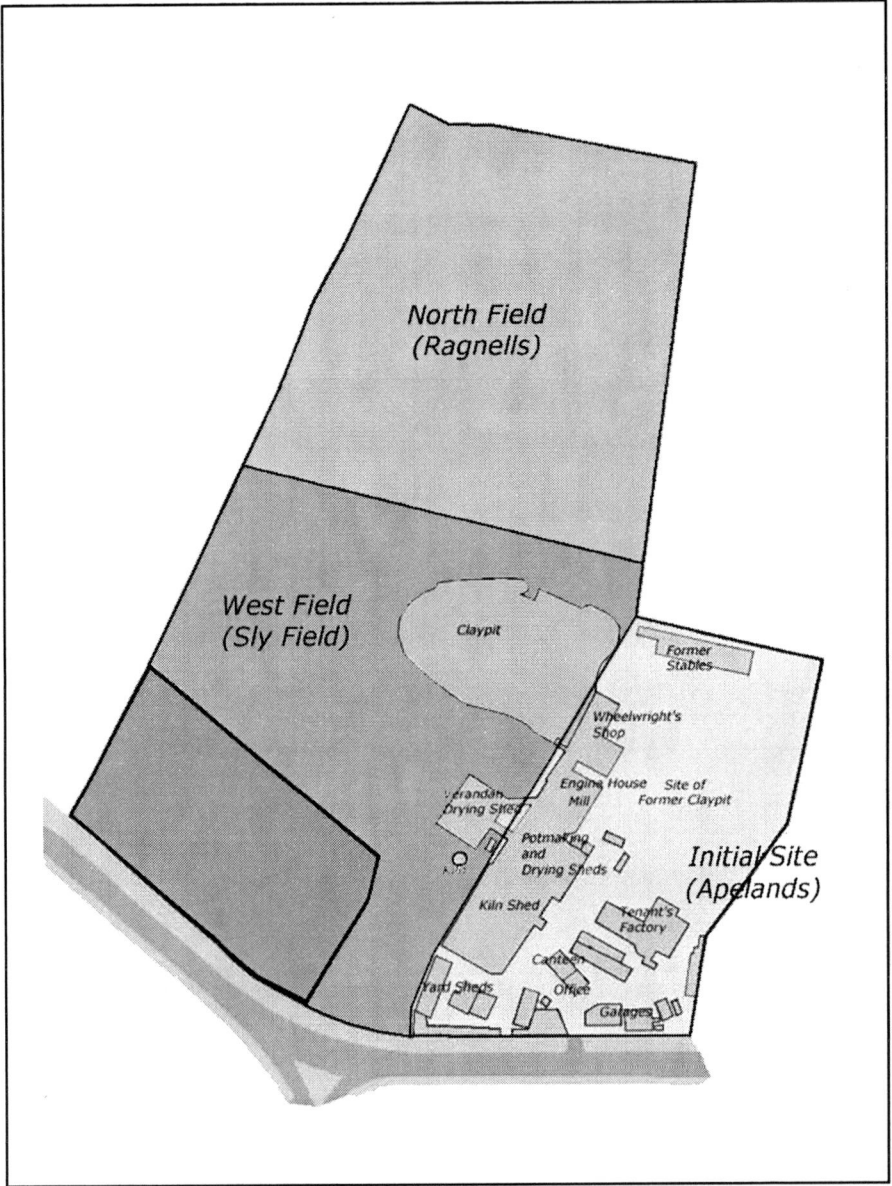

North Field
(Ragnells)

West Field
(Sly Field)

Claypit

Former
Stables

Wheelwright's
Shop

Engine House   Site of
Mill   Former Claypit

Verandah
Drying Sheds

Potmaking
and
Drying Sheds

Kiln

Initial Site
(Apelands)

Kiln Shed

Tenant's
Factory

Canteen

Yard Sheds

Office

Garages

White Hart Lane pottery site 1948
Based on plan prepared by H. Seymour Couchman & Sons

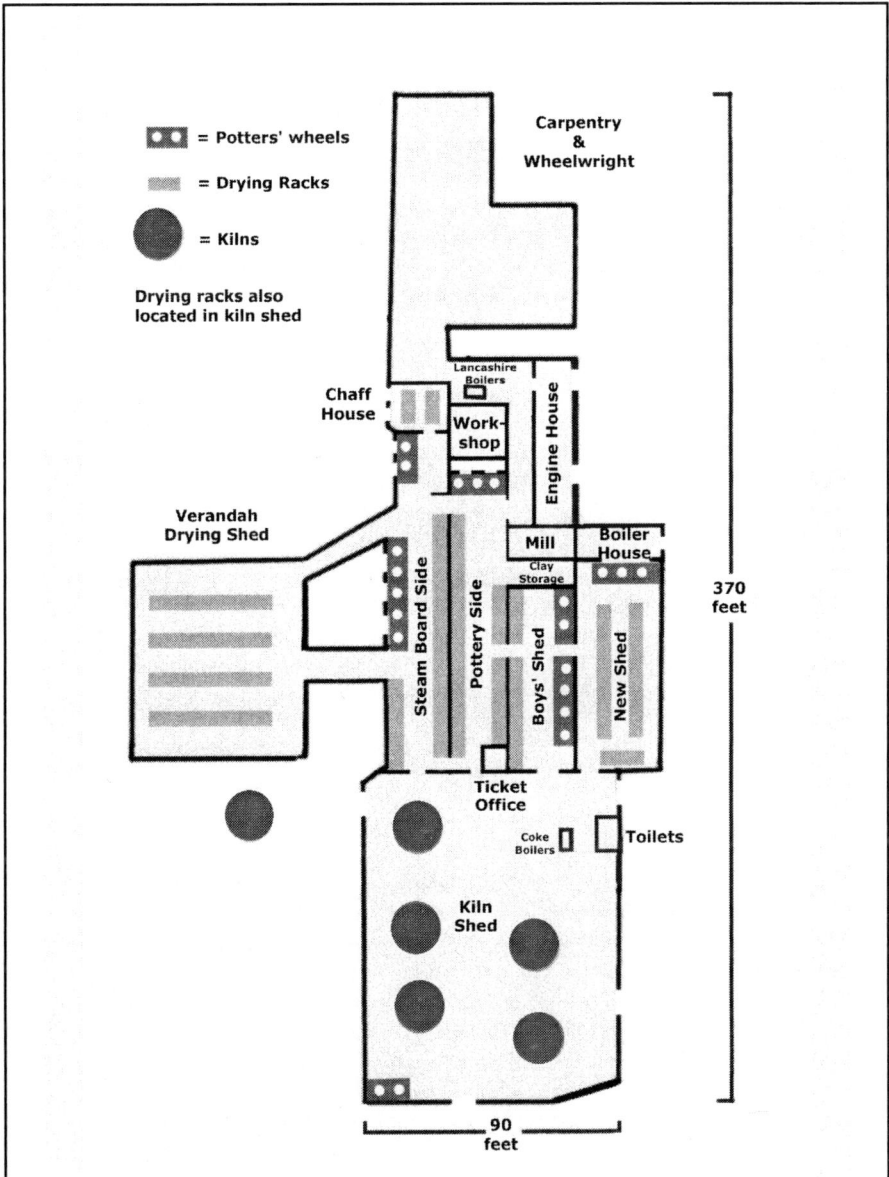

Plan of potmaking, drying and kiln sheds 1960
White Hart Lane pottery

Potmaker circa 1955

One of the drying sheds 1960

One of the kilns 1927

Loading flowerpots circa 1955

New steam engine being installed 1935
Samuel South(2) far right Charles South (son) in background

"Atora" bullock wagon at White Hart Lane pottery 1937
Samuel South(2) right

Part Two
The Potteries

Angel Road Pottery
1868-1886

1868 - 1874

Throughout the journey southwards from Barley, the birth registrations of his children record the occupation of Joseph as a brickmaker. The bulk and weight of bricks rendered transport over long distances impracticable and manufacture usually took place at local brickworks or on building sites themselves. Bricks were moulded from the brickearth excavated during the construction works and fired in makeshift kilns. The pug mill used to breakdown and mix the clay would be a portable item of equipment comprising an upright cylinder with an internal roller that was turned by a horse walking in a circular path around it. It was a strenuous life working in the open in all weathers.

The arrival of Joseph and his family in Edmonton coincided with the expansion of the district as transport links improved. Horse buses provided regular services to London and the railways, which had arrived in 1840, communicated directly with the capital by 1871[1]. Between 1861 and 1901 the population of Edmonton increased four-fold[2]. The resultant demand for housing would have created an acute need for building materials. During the second half of the 19th century brickfields in the Edmonton area would have provided employment for Joseph's skills. He also introduced his sons to the trade. The 1861 census records his two elder sons, Joseph(2), aged 10 and Solomon, aged 9, as "Working in a Brickfield", presumably with their father.

During the same period there was a significant expansion of the Lea Valley nursery industry[3]. The River Lea flows from south Hertfordshire, through north and east London before discharging into the River Thames. Nurserymen had been attracted to the valley because of the fertile soil, the plentiful supply of water, the proximity of London and the good transport links. The industry flourished between the mid nineteenth and mid twentieth centuries and at its peak boasted that it had the largest area of land under glass in the world.

There were concentrations of nurseries in the Hackney, Tottenham and Edmonton districts. Residential and industrial development of these areas in the later nineteenth century caused the nurserymen to move northwards to the cleaner air of south east Hertfordshire. Also, the increase in the value of the land for building use would have imposed economic pressures. The success of the nursery industry created an enormous demand for clay flower pots; a fact that did not escape the notice of Joseph, and in 1868[4] he founded a small pottery in Water Lane, Edmonton.

Water Lane[5], later Angel Road, extended eastwards from Fore Street to the River Lea Navigation. At the time the pottery was established, there were a few houses in Water Lane near the ribbon development of Fore Street but extensive residential development took place over the ensuing years. Despite the development, the lane remained unmade and in a poor state of repair and was subjected to frequent flooding from Pymmes Brook which ran along its northern boundary. The flooding made the lane impassable and on occasion entered the neighbouring properties.

The pottery land was leased from a Mr. Atkin[6] and was located to the south of Angel Road midway between the junctions with Fore Street and Dysons Lane (later Road). According to the 1884 Edmonton Rating valuations the premises comprised "Cottage Stables and Pot Manufactory". It seems that after his marriage to Mary Ann Dutton, Joseph moved into the cottage and the 1871 Census records his address as "19 Angel Road or Water Lane", which was the last house before the Dysons Lane junction. The second child of the marriage, Florence, however, was born away from Angel Road in 1873 at Frederick Place, Lower Fore Street.

An uncertainty arises with regard to the introduction of the South family to the pottery industry. Whilst the processing of clay into a workable state and the control of kilns during firing are similar to both brick and pot making, nevertheless, the skill required to "throw" a pot is entirely different from the moulding of bricks and would involve tuition to acquire "the art". There is no current record that Joseph was other than a brickmaker which is the occupation shown in each census and each registration certificate. In all of the records subsequent to 1868 which have been inspected he continues to describe himself as a brickmaker. The description is entered on the 1871 census and his eldest son, Joseph (aged 21), is also listed as a brickmaker. Samuel(1) (aged 18) appears as a labourer and Solomon was serving in the army. Joseph junior is recorded as "Brickmaker and Potter" for the first time on the registration certificate of his second child, Florence, in October 1874 and Samuel(1) as a "Potter" at his 1875 marriage. Whether Joseph senior acquired an existing business or founded a new venture, whether he ever worked as a potter and where Joseph and Samuel(1) learnt their potmaking skills, are all questions that remain unresolved.

In the weeks leading up to the departure of Joseph from the UK there was an important decision to be made regarding the future of the pottery. Joseph decided to sell the business to his third son, Samuel(1). Father and son met on the 3 February 1874 to complete the sale. Daniel Dutton, the father of Mary Ann, was also present and acted as witness. An inventory of the plant and stock was taken, the price agreed, and a sale document drawn up in Joseph's hand[7]. Interestingly, the horse needed to drive the pugmill and deliver the pots is not included in the sale. Perhaps it was sold separately by Joseph.

I Joseph South Sen do agree to sell to Samuel South the undermentioned Pots Plants and etc of the Pottery Angel Road Middx

30 cast 60 pots at 1s 2d	£1	15s	0d
Tumble cart	£3	00s	0d
Pugmill	£3	00s	0d
Old van and harness	£2	00s	0d
2 spindles and Boards	£4	00s	0d
Pot Kiln	£4	00s	0d
Small stump of fodder	£1	10s	0d
	£22	5s	0d	[£22.25]

Paid   Joseph South sen.
Witness Daniel Dutton

The total is incorrect and should be £19 5s. 0d. [£19.25]. It is to be hoped that the error was inadvertent and not a deliberate attempt by the father to defraud his son. Joseph departed for New Zealand the following month and Samuel(1) was now owner of the pottery.

1874 - 1886

It could have been expected that Joseph would favour his eldest son and namesake who was aged 24 and already married. Joseph junior clearly had ambition to manage his own business rather than be in the employ of others as demonstrated by his later career. The decision to sell the pottery to Samuel(1) becomes less understandable because after the departure of his father, Joseph junior moved into the cottage at the pottery where his second child was born in October 1874. At that time his occupation was that of brickmaker and potter which infers that he was working at the pottery now owned by his younger brother. If clues are sought for proof of family tensions then the sale to the younger son could be evidence of a rift between Joseph and his eldest son.

After his own marriage in 1875 Samuel(1) took up residence at 26 Angel Road Terrace, a terrace of recently built houses and a very short walk to the pottery. By 1878, Joseph junior had left the pottery cottage for a house and shop in Upper Fore Street, Edmonton, and gave up working as a potter. The cottage was then occupied by his parents-in-law, James and Eliza Webb, and their son, William (later to become foreman at Joseph's brickfield), who were living at the address as late as 1891. Curiously, the surviving records of the Edmonton Rating Valuations continue to identify Joseph junior as the registered occupier of the pottery premises up to at least 1884.

Selection of the site in Angel Road was a wise decision. Over the following years a number of nurseries were established in the Angel Road and Dysons Lane area by Edward Chidley, Joseph Dent, John Edden, H. B. May, R. H. May, G. Poulton, and J. Tyler[1]. Customers for flower pots were literally 'on the door step'. With the exception of Chidley and R. H. May, Samuel South(1) supplied all of these nurserymen.

At the time of the 1881 Census Samuel(1) is described as a "Potter employing 3 men and 2 boys" and interesting insights into the pottery of this period are available from the pottery sales ledger for the years 1882 – 1887 held in the archives at Bruce Castle Museum, Tottenham[2]. The ledger records 36 customers together with the size, quantity and cost of pots delivered to them. The business was conducted on a credit basis. There are examples in the ledger of deliveries to a customer over several months before payment is made. With two exceptions, all of the customers were located in either Edmonton or Tottenham. The hand written entries were made by Samuel(1) and demonstrate that he was a poor speller, for example, "Winchmoor [Winchmore] Hill", "Disons [Dysons] Road", "Tomas [Thomas] Green". Bearing in mind the elementary nature of the education that he had received, these errors are, perhaps, understandable (and excusable).

A typical entry is that recording sales to the nursery of Henry Cull & George Rooke in Northumberland Park:

Date	Quantity	Size	Cost
January 1884			
26	35 cast	48	£2 – 00s – 10d
	20 cast	L 60	£1 – 00s – 00d
28	40 cast	48	£2 – 06s – 08d
31	80 cast	L 60	£4 – 00s – 00d
February 1884			
4	50 cast	48	£2 – 18s – 04d
15	50 cast	48	£2 – 18s – 04d
March 1884			
1	50 cast	L 60	£2 – 10s – 00d
	20 cast	48	£1 – 03s – 04d
	10 cast	48	£0 – 11s – 08d
(no date)	25 cast	Thumbs	£1 – 02s – 11d

The entry on 26 January 1884 for 20 cast of large 60's represents 1200 pots sold at a cost of one pound and the equivalent of the daily output of a "good" potter. There are also examples of the entrepreneurial spirit of Samuel(1). He sold "manuer" (presumably from the horse used to deliver the pots) at 4s. [20p] for each "load carted" and the horse and cart was hired out at 9s. [45p] per day.

The opening and closing periods of the ledger are for part years only and the rounded sales recorded for complete periods are:

1883	£480
1884	£465
1885	£400
1886	£430

An 1884 report into the "Wages and Earnings of the Working Classes"[3] records that average weekly wages for "highly skilled artisans" was 30s. to 40s. [£1.50 to £2.00]; "less skilled" earned 23s. to 28s. [£1.15 to £1.40]; and "common labourers" were paid 15s. to 20s. [75p. to £1.00]. A specific example is given for potters ("throwers") employed in the Midlands who received 7s. [35p] a day [£1.925 for a 5½ day week]. Arguably, less expertise is required to make the utilitarian flower pot than the finer products of the ceramic industry and the South potters were more likely to be at the lower end of the skilled workers earnings range. An annual income of some £75 may reasonably be presumed.

The job allocation of the "three men and two boys" mentioned in the 1881 census can only be speculated but assuming that two were working as potters and taking the "two boys" as equivalent to an adult, the following wage bill is extrapolated:

2 Potters (highly skilled)	@	£75	=	£150
1 labourer	@	£50	=	£50
2 boys (equal 1 labourer)	@	£50	=	£50
				£250

A potential wage roll of £250 per annum is sufficient, based on the recorded sales, for a profitable business after allowance for his own earnings and overheads. The experience that Samuel(1) had gained managing the small pottery would have proved invaluable when he later expanded his business interests.

From the period covered by the ledger there is evidence of a regular and stable customer base and, of course, the nursery industry continued to expand. The resources available at the Angel Road Pottery to exploit and profit from such expansion were, however, limited. The clay soil on the site was not ideal for potmaking and the business relied heavily on external supplies of clay which were obtained from material excavated on local building sites and also from burials[4]. There can be small doubt that Samuel(1) was aware of events that were happening less than two miles away in White Hart Lane, Tottenham, and when the opportunity arose to expand the business he grasped it.

White Hart Lane Pottery
1886-1960

1886-1919

By 1886 there were two potteries occupying adjacent sites in White Hart Lane. One was in the ownership of Edward Cole, a local potter, and the other occupied by Richard Sankey, a potmaker from Bulwell, Nottingham. Sankey had tried to undercut Cole but was unsuccessful and retreated to his Bulwell base[1]. In 1886 Samuel South(1), limited by the resources of his Angel Road pottery, seized the opportunity to expand and transferred his business to the site, taking over the lease, and continuing to employ some of the former Sankey employees[2]. He also moved his family into one of the pair of houses that stood adjacent to the entrance to the Cole pottery[3]. His rival potmaker lived next door[4].

The South connection with Sankey continued over the ensuing years. Both became fellow members of the National Association of Horticultural Pottery Manufacturers which was established to protect the interests of the industry. In the 1920s, Samuel(1)'s grandson, Samuel(3), served a form of apprentice-ship at the Bulwell pottery before joining the family business. In later years, the South pottery bought in ornamental pots, no longer made by them, from Sankey. The firm of Sankey survives today, although no longer under family ownership, and their range of plastic pots and other garden accessories will be familiar to garden centre visitors.

When Samuel(1) arrived at White Hart Lane the pottery consisted of a single shed and two kilns[5]. Without main drainage or artificial lighting, working conditions were harsh[6]. Work was carried out by candlelight and other illumination came from coke braziers, oil lamps or, simply, the glare of the kiln fires[7]. The journey to work meant a long walk along an unmade, unlit, hedge-lined country lane with very few houses. Often the men brought their food to work in a pudding basin, tied up in a handkerchief, to heat on the kiln fires[8].

A period of rapid expansion followed and by the mid 1890s there was a workforce of over 80 men[9]. Samuel(1) invested heavily in the business. In 1896 he purchased a steam powered clay mill (£150) and pug mill (£25) from William Boulton of the Providence Foundry, Burslem[10]. The total account, with accessories and other fittings, amounted to £250. 5s. 8d. [£250.29]. Boulton was a leading manufacturer of pottery machinery and an 1893 trade journal article reported[11];

"Another machine of Mr. Boulton's, which has considerably improved the quality of the clay, and dispensed with a good deal of hard labour, which frequently fell upon juveniles, is the pug mill for consolidating the clay."

Potters' wheels were also purchased from Boulton[12] and the South pottery was thus equipped with the latest machinery.

The expansion of the White Hart Lane Potteries after the arrival of Samuel South(1) is illustrated by his bank book[13] for the period June 1886 – September 1892 which has survived. The account was held with the Tottenham branch of the London & Provincial Bank Ltd and the passbook, similar to a bank statement, records each deposit made (amount only) and each cheque drawn (amount and payee). All but 9 of the 360 deposit entries are for cash receipts. Out-goings recorded include payments to Rickett (coal merchant), Stockbridge (coal merchant), Boulton (engineer) and Chesser (farrier). The first three payments between 29 July 1886 - 5 August 1886 totalling £55 were made to Sankey, perhaps, for the purchase of plant and the like from him.

The total amounts paid into the accounts for the years 1887-1892 were:

Year	Receipts
1887	£1028
1888	£1958
1889	£2259
1890	£2270
1891	£2912
1892 (Jan-Sept - projected pro-rata)	£3597

Turnover had increased threefold over a period of six years and almost eight times the sales recorded at the Angel Road pottery ten years previously. The results are even more impressive because Sankey had withdrawn, unable to make the pottery pay. The income was likely to have been more than recorded because the business was primarily conducted in cash and monies received could be used to meet outgoings without passing through the account.

Protection of the environment is not an exclusive 21st century concern. In the 1890s, the Inspector of Nuisances employed by the Wood Green Council made frequent visits to White Hart Lane in order to record the smoke emissions from the kilns and engine houses of the South and Cole potteries although there were few houses in the immediate area. A watch was kept for periods up to an hour and his journals meticulously record when and for how long black smoke was emitted. Following visits in February and March 1897, a Statutory Notice to abate the nuisance was served on each pottery owner[14]. Samuel(1) and Edward Cole both wrote to the Local Authority confirming that they were prepared and willing to take such steps needed to alleviate the position[15]. The official action seems to have had the desired effect. At an inspection carried out on 25 May 1897 the Inspector noted no smoke from the South pottery and only slight smoke from the Cole premises but over the ensuing months denser, black, smoke is recorded once again[16].

By 1894[17] there was a collection of buildings including the pottery office and a larger covered area over the potmaking and drying sheds together with four outside kilns. Development of the site continued progressively and planning permission was obtained in 1906[18] to construct additional stabling providing accommodation for 20 horses. By 1913[19] the number of outbuildings on the site had increased significantly although the kilns remained uncovered.

There were, in the opening decade of the 20th century, proposals that, if implemented, would have had a dramatic effect on the future of the pottery. In this period there was a growth in the promotion of underground railways in the London area. The Hammersmith, City & North East London Railway line was proposed in 1903[20], 1905[21] and 1906[22] with a route northwards from London and terminating in either Palmers Green or Southgate. A surface section of all three railways was planned to pass completely through the Tottenham Potteries of E G Cole & Son and the eastern part of the South & Sons' pottery[23]. The survey accompanying the plans for the projected route identifies Joseph Schonfield as the owner of the land and Samuel South(1) and Edward Cole as the lessees and occupiers. Whether

63

the South pottery would have been a viable proposition after construction of the railway can only be a topic for speculation but, in any event, none of the proposed railways proceeded.

Like any successful businessman Samuel(1) fostered a close relationship with his major customers, the nurserymen of the Lea Valley. He accompanied a party of nurserymen to the USA[24]in 1911 visiting American cities including Baltimore. A similar trip was made in 1914 to the Dutch bulb fields[25]. Promotional gifts were given out to customers. An ornamental earthenware plinth and urn presented in 1912 to nurseryman George Rooke, a customer from the days of the Angel Road pottery, remained on display in the garden of his grandson, Peter Rooke, in 2000[26].

The South businesses of potmaking, brickmaking, cartage and property were managed from the modest office which, up to the closure of the pottery in 1960, retained a Dickensian air. A high, sloping, desk with brass fittings, which had been purchased from a City shipping firm[27], ran along the front wall of the general office supporting massive ledgers. A small side room, furnished with an impressive roll-top desk, was used by Samuel(1) for the conduct of his business affairs[28]. Samuel South & Sons was amongst the first subscribers to the Tottenham telephone exchange and was allocated number 54, which continued in use until 1934 when the connection was replaced with Bowes Park 4047[29].

Up to one hundred horses[30], stabled at the pottery, were used to draw the delivery wagons and for the cartage business which became the prime activity between 1898-1909[31]. The number of horses and wagons required the services of a wheelwright, harness maker and blacksmith who were all pottery employees[32]. Maud Hickson, a grand-daughter of Samuel(1), has recalled accompanying her father, John South, on Sunday outings to the pottery where he would walk through the stables to check on the horses and also visit the kiln shed to inspect the kilns being fired[33].

Each of Samuel(1)'s six sons had joined their father in his businesses. John, Arthur and Alfred, saw service during World War 1. Samuel(2), aged 38 when war was declared, was managing the pottery, Walter[34]and Charles [35] suffering from poor health, remained. The three serving sons returned safely although Alfred stayed in France after the armistice and he was unable to attend his father's funeral in 1919[36]. During the war pottery horses were requisitioned by the Government[37] and the depletion of the workforce caused manning difficulties at the pottery. Local boy scouts helped to monitor the kilns[38] and Samuel(2)'s daughter, Hilda, assisted in the pottery office[39].

It was whilst visiting the pottery office on the morning of New Year's Day, 1919 that Samuel(1) was taken ill[40]. He died, over night, in his sleep, and the first chapter in the history of the White Hart Lane pottery came to a close.

1919-1930

After the death of his father, Samuel(2) purchased the pottery business from the Estate and relinquished his interest in the remainder of the trust established under the will. His brothers, John and Charles remained with the business whilst Walter, Arthur and Alfred left to establish South Brothers[1], builders.

A war surplus 3 ton Pierce-Arrow[2] motor lorry was acquired in 1921[3] and was driven by John South who had learnt to drive in the army[4]. The open cockpit was simply protected with a folding canopy and the pottery carpenter constructed an enclosed cab with decorative fretting over the windscreen[5]. There were no doors but a waist high fixed board on the offside afforded some protection to the driver whilst the nearside access was completely open to the elements[6]. Over the coming years motor transport gradually replaced horse power although two horses were retained and used to cart coal from Noel Park Railway Station[7]. The value of this mode of transport was demonstrated when, during the petrol shortages of the Second World War, Whitbread, the brewers, hired the horses to deliver beer barrels to the local public houses[8].

A series of publicity postcards was published in the 1920s illustrated with different scenes of the pottery and boasting that Samuel South & Sons were the "largest makers of horticultural pottery in England". The claim clearly did not meet with the approval of rival potmakers and, even in the days before the Advertising Standards Authority, the postcards were then over-printed with the prefix "one of"[9]. Developments during this period included the erection of a further drying shed[10] on the neighbouring land that had been acquired[11], old kilns were rebuilt and new kilns erected[12].

The sons of Samuel(2) were expected to join their father in the family business and by 1927 Samuel(3)[13] was working at the pottery to be followed in turn by his younger brothers Charles and Ted. Jim South, however, entered the nursery industry. A son-in-law, Reg Scapens, husband of Elsie South, worked for a time as a driver at the pottery[14].

Samuel(3) became production manager[15] responsible for kilns, yardmen and drivers with Charles as "superintendent of making"[16] in charge of the potmakers and clay pit. At about this time, John South decided to leave the pottery[17] although his brother, Charles, continued to act as the salesman representative and made good use of his extensive contacts throughout the nursery industry and at Covent Garden market[18]. Later, Joyce, youngest daughter of Samuel(2), came to work in the pottery office[19].

1930-1940
Business at the pottery flourished in the 1930s and a newspaper article[1] appeared in the second half of the decade enquiring "What is the secret of the growing prosperity of British flower-pot manufacturers?" It went on to consider the industry's claim that they were "increasing their business every month; paying wages which rank among the highest in any industry in Great Britain; and reducing foreign competition to a minimum." Sidney Cole of E. G. Cole & Son, the neighbouring and rival pottery, commented *"We are benefiting from protection which is now being given to nurserymen in this country. The duties which have been placed on imported pot-plants has restored confidence among English growers and some are now ordering flower-pots by the 100,000".*

Development of the South pottery site continued. By 1935 there were 7 kilns, six of which were entirely enclosed within a kiln shed[2]. A new steam engine to drive the mill and potters' wheels was installed in 1935[3]; a further drying shed was erected in 1938; the last (and largest) kiln was built in 1939[4]; and a canteen built for the pottery workers[5]. The opportunity for an unusual diversification arose when Atora, producers of beef suet, used a colourful covered wagon drawn by a pair of horned bullocks in a long running publicity campaign[6]. When the wagon visited North London the bullocks were housed in the former stables at the pottery[7]. Straw and accommodation was also provided for animal acts that performed at the Wood Green Empire[8].

In 1931, Samuel(2) contributed towards the cost of a drinking fountain in White Hart Lane, close to the pottery, which Wood Green Council had decided to erect for the benefit of passers-by[9]. A "hearty vote of thanks" was passed by the councillors[10]. Unfortunately, the fountain was the subject of vandalism and frequently out of action[11]. By 1932 the Council were considering the removal of the installation with the approval of Samuel(2) who agreed that it was a source of annoyance[12].

An industrial dispute with the potmakers occurred in November 1936 and the progress of the strike was reported in "The Weekly Herald"[13]. The dispute started on 10 November when a batch of saucers made by one of the potters was ordered to be destroyed as unsuitable because of poor workmanship and for which he would receive no payment. He claimed that some of the saucers were good and, refusing to comply with the instruction, he was sacked. Later in the day, 13 potters went on strike in sympathy and were joined by another five men within a few days. A further 13 non-union potters remained at work.

The strikers claimed that the incident was not unique and instructions for the destruction of good product had been issued over a period of time. For their part, the Souths denied the charge saying it was absurd that they would require good saucers to be smashed. The dispute received the backing of the Transport and General Workers' Union and the pottery entrance was picketed. On 30 November the union wrote to the firm setting out their demands and inviting negotiations. The approach was rejected and "Mr. South told the 'Weekly Herald'" that "*Their terms were disagreeable to us and we have done nothing about it.* Over the period of the strike, three of the strikers had returned to work and the newspaper later reported that the remaining men were to return to work on Saturday, 30 November. The terms of the settlement, if any, were not reported.

During the inter war years Samuel(2) indulged his interest of raising pigs in sties erected next to the stables. When one of the stable blocks became redundant it was converted into a piggery. He often surprised business acquaintances with his knowledge of porcine husbandry[14]. The collection of livestock was completed by a flock of geese[15] which were regarded as better security than any guard dog.

This successful period, however, was brought to an abrupt halt by the outbreak of the Second World War. Within days of the declaration of war on 3 September 1939 there was an indication of the difficulties that were to be encountered in attempting to continue the normal production of the pottery. Stringent regulations had been imposed prohibiting the emission of lights during Blackout periods which could act as navigational aids to enemy aircraft. On 15 September the Wood Green Weekly Herald reported:

"Because of the danger of flames being spotted, the kilns of the White Hart-lane Potteries have been damped down on the instructions of the police."

Attempts to comply with the regulations were unsuccessful. With the departure of men from the pottery into the forces and the inability to shield the glare from the kilns, it was decided to close the business down for the duration except for essential maintenance[16]. Orders were fulfilled from a stock pile of 8,000,000 pots that had been counted in the yards in 1939[17]. Some deliveries were being made as late as 1945[18].

The three sons of Samuel(2) working at the pottery enlisted and served overseas; Samuel(3) with the Royal Artillery in Burma and Charles with the Royal Electrical and Mechanical Engineers in Italy. Ted South, a sapper in the Royal Engineers, received fatal wounds during the retreat to Dunkirk.

1940-1960
The pottery re-opened after the war but never recovered fully from the closure. There was a shortage of skilled potters; increased labour costs; significantly increased costs of coal, which was subject to shortages; a gradual decline in the nursery industry and the introduction of machine made pots and plastic pots by their larger competitors Sankey and Ward. Machine made pots which were 30% cheaper to produce than hand thrown pots were considered by the Souths to be an inferior product being less durable and porous[1]. Made under pressure, the pots were disposed to de-laminate and suffer frost damage[2].

With an individual kiln consuming between 8-10 tons during each firing, the difficulties encountered with coal supply were particularly damaging and threatened a complete stoppage of production. Interviewed in April 1947[3] Charles South explained:

"We are allocated less than ten tons a week - enough for two days' work. We cannot carry on at that rate. We were just beginning to get started again after the war-time close-down and our staff are returning from the Services to find that we cannot give them a full week's work. The demand for fruit and vegetable growing is unprecedented but we cannot supply a fraction of it".

Not all potters returned to the pottery after the war[4]. The reduction of output caused by the fuel shortages affected their piece work earnings and employment in other trades became more attractive. Over the post war years some 40 recruits were taken on as trainee potmakers but could only be paid a basic wage until they were sufficiently experienced to produce satisfactory pots for sale. Even those considered suitable to become potters found that unskilled jobs could be obtained for a higher wage than the earnings available during their training. In addition, many did not return after the two years National Service which was compulsory from the age of eighteen.

To overcome the shortage of skilled labour, Samuel(3) and Charles returned to the potter's wheel and even their father, now in his seventies, returned to the craft that he had learnt some 60 years before[5]. His grandsons, Peter and Graham, joined the South pottery in the early 1950s and became the fifth generation of Souths to be engaged in the clay industry. Graham South visited the pottery of Richard Sankey at Bulwell, Nottinghamshire, to inspect the process for machine made pots[6]. Test equipment was purchased and installed at the White Hart Lane Potteries but the clay on the site was found to be unsuitable for the process, a denser material was needed, and it was decided not to invest in the venture[7].

In 1953 the Waltham Abbey pottery of G & A Tuck followed the example of Souths and replaced their steam engine, which provided power to the machinery, with an electric motor[8]. Some difficulty was encountered and the mill was out of action for three weeks although there was only sufficient processed clay to last the potmakers for two weeks. The South pottery provided the clay for the remaining period to enable production to continue.

Since the Angel Road pottery was founded in 1868 each successive business had been in sole ownership with the attendant rights and liabilities. Samuel(2) reached his 70th birthday in 1946 and the potential level of death duties on his estate would impose a heavy financial burden possibly resulting in the sale of the pottery to meet the liability. In order to protect the family business, Samuel South & Sons became a limited company capitalised with 20,000 1s 0d ordinary shares allocated as follows[9]:

Samuel South(3)	9250 shares
Charles South	9250 shares
Samuel South(2)	1000 shares
Emily Maud South	500 shares

Samuel(2) had effectively passed ownership of the pottery to his sons although retaining sufficient shares to have a casting vote should this become necessary. After the expiry of the seven year qualifying period required for the transfer of ownership to be entirely exempt from tax liability he celebrated the occasion by giving £5 to each of his 17 grandchildren[10]. The wisdom of the decision to create a limited company was proven within a few years when Samuel South(2) died on the 16 June 1956. His shares were bequeathed to Samuel(3) (500 shares), Charles South (250 shares) and his daughter, Hilda Beech (250 shares).

Nurserymen continued to be the prime market for South pots and the Stuart Low nursery of Bush Hill Park, Enfield, reputed to be the largest operation of its type in the UK, was one of the customers[11]. The customer base, however, had broadened and included twelve parks maintained by London County Council, Chessington Zoo, various Local Authorities and Hospital Trusts[12]. But the nursery industry was also facing difficulties and experiencing increases in labour costs[13]. Improvements in cultivation techniques made nurserymen less dependent on the fertile soil of the Lea Valley and the availability of piped water lessened the reliance on well supplies. More efficient oil fired heating systems were replacing the need for coal carried by the Lea Navigation barges and, not least, the importation of cheaper foreign produce was on the increase. All of these adverse factors culminated in 1951 when large tracts of land in Waltham Cross and Cheshunt were re-designated for housing.

Despite the continuing customer base it was apparent that the day of mass produced hand thrown flower pots had passed. Competition created by the introduction of machine made and plastic pots was further compounded. In 1955 a change in the tax laws resulted in the imposition of a 30% Purchase Tax on hand made pottery. The topic was the subject of correspondence to The Times newspaper which, on 17 March 1955, published a letter, from Sidney Cole, the owner of the neighbouring pottery, E. G. Cole & Son. He wrote that "*the purchase tax will make it [potmaking] uneconomical and have ceased production this week.* Despite these comments, the Cole pottery continued production until 1957. In addition, the introduction of the 1956 Clean Air Act which sought to control smoke emissions from residential and industrial premises placed an additional burden on the operation of the pottery.

Any future development or diversification of the South business would require significant investment that was beyond the resources of the company without substantial borrowings[14]. Samuel(3) commented "*If the firm contemplated expansion it would have to come from new capital*"[15] Other local potters had arrived at the same decision and in addition to the closure of the Cole pottery, Pettitt & Son in Walthamstow had not reopened after the Second World War[16]and G. & A. Tuck at Waltham Abbey was to close in 1963[17].

Samuel(3) and his brother, Charles, decided to sell the White Hart Lane pottery land. In an interview[18]after the closure Samuel(2) explained the impact of rising costs on the business:

"*People expect to pay more for a suit or a car than they did before the war. But they do not find it so easy to understand why flowerpots should be affected by the spiral trend. Yet the coal we used to buy for 26 shillings in 1939 eventually cost us £6 12s.*"

Wedlake Saint & Co., solicitors, and Couchmans, surveyors, were retained as advisers[19]. The value of the company lay in the freehold land owned by it and not the plant, stock and goodwill of the pottery business. Counsel's

Opinion was obtained as to the most efficient method of sale and the decision was reached to sell the company and its assets rather than disposal of the land as separate entity. An offer of £180,000 made in June 1960 from Idris Ltd, soft drink manufacturers (shortly to become part of the Beecham Group), was accepted. The shareholders of Samuel South & Sons Co. Ltd. and their representatives met in October 1960 and the formal transfer documents signed. After payment of solicitor's and surveyor's fees the purchase sum was distributed proportionally to the number of shares held. At the insistence of the two South brothers the following clause was inserted in the sale document:

"At the request of the Vendors the name of the Company will be changed making no use of the words 'Samuel South & Sons' and no restriction will be placed on the use by the Vendors of that name should they so wish."

Potmaking ceased on 5 October, 1960. There was no statutory requirement for redundancy compensation but payments of up to £100 each was made to the employees. The last pots thrown by four of the potters were inscribed and donated to Bruce Castle Museum in Tottenham. Graham South, however, was determined to throw the very last pot. Waiting until the potmakers' shed was clear, he returned and made a '48' pot; the last pot thrown at White Hart Lane[20]. The story of the pottery business established by Joseph South 92 years earlier had finally come to a close.

White Hart Lane Site

The site that the pottery of Samuel South & Sons eventually came to occupy at White Hart Lane was acquired by them in three separate transactions over a period of some years.

Initial Site

Lying to the north of White Hart Lane, and mid-way between Tottenham High Road and the hamlet of Wood Green, were two adjoining fields mentioned in the ancient Manor Rolls of Tottenham and described in the 1619 Earl of Dorset Survey as "Two closes of arrable [sic] and pasture grounds called Apelands". By the mid 19th century the fields were the site of Tent Farm owned by the Kenworthy family[1]. The land overlaid rich deposits of London clay and it was not long before this natural resource was being exploited.

Edward Cole was leasing the eastern field for use as a pottery by 1876 and Samuel Johnson, a brickmaker, was occupying the field to the west[2]. The fields of Devonshire Hill Farm, owned by the New River Company, lay to the north and west of the site. In a survey undertaken for the Company in 1870, their agent noted that brick making was being carried on in an adjoining field[3]. Although documentation of his occupation of the site is lacking, there is no doubt, from the recorded recollections of members of the South and Cole families, that Richard Sankey followed Johnson onto the site and commenced making pots in competition with E. G. Cole & Son[4].

After the departure of Sankey, Samuel South(1) took over the lease and in 1886 was occupying the 5 acres which continued to be described as a "brickground"[5]. By 1903 the land was owned by Elizabeth Kenworthy[6], who died the following year. Although her brother-in-law, Joshua Schonfield, is recorded as having ownership in 1904[7], nevertheless, the available rating records continue to list a member of the Kenworthy family as owner for some years. It was not until 1922 that Samuel South(2) was able to purchase the land from the Public Trustee[8].

West Field

Another ancient field, Sly[1] (or Stye[2]) Field, of some 5 acres, lay to the west of the pottery site. It had been acquired by the London County Council in 1901[3] as part of a much larger estate intended for housing development. The land, however, became surplus to their requirements. In 1914, with the intention of using the land for future clay workings Couchmans, the advisers of Samuel South(1), approached the LCC enquiring whether they would be prepared to dispose of the land to him[4]. After negotiations a sale was agreed in the sum of £1,800 together with the exchange of two parcels of land, totalling 4½ acres, to the north of nearby Devonshire Hill Lane that were owned by Samuel(1)[5].

Part of the field was sold by Samuel South(2) to R. Strawbridge Ltd., bakers, in 1936[6] and the Wonderloaf bakery was built on the site[7]. Reece Strawbridge had founded a small bakery and shop in Green Lanes, Palmers Green, and went on to open other retail outlets in the area[8]. The bakery erected in White Hart Lane was a substantial building with an art deco façade and well tended gardens along the frontage[9]. Strawbridge is credited with the introduction of sliced, wrapped, bread into the UK[10].

Relations with their neighbour were sometimes strained. One hot summer's day in the 1950s the windows in the bakery were left open for ventilation but the direction of the wind changed and smoke from the kilns entered the bakery ruining the day's production[11]. In high dudgeon, a representative from the bakery called at the pottery requesting compensation. Samuel South(3) forcibly replied that the kilns were present before the bakery and nothing further was heard. The opportunity to turn the tables arose when Wonderloaf built an extension to their premises on the boundary with the South property. After building works were completed Samuel(3) pointed out to Wonderloaf that the foundations encroached onto the South land and requested that the offending wall should be removed. A rental payment was offered by the bakery although the final outcome is unknown. The wall remained in position and it is likely that Samuel(3) achieved sufficient satisfaction from the discomforture experienced by the Wonderloaf management.

In 1955, a small parcel of land abutting the eastern boundary of the Wonderloaf site was sold to C. McNab Mackintosh Ltd, trading as the Regent Garage, and a service station was built[12].

North Field

Ragnells[1] (or Raylands[2]), a field of seven acres which adjoined the northern boundary of the pottery site, had been acquired by the New River Company in 1839[3] and annexed to their Clay Hill Farm (later Devonshire Hill) Farm land. The farmhouse was the family home of Samuel South(1) for a short period and, after his death in 1919, the lease of the holding was taken over by Samuel(2).

The New River Company embarked on a policy of disposing of the farm and in 1928 Samuel(2) purchased 22 acres of the land, including the former Ragnells for the sum £9,000[4]. Of this land, some 15 acres was sold by him in 1934[5] and 1935[6] for housing developments. The remaining acres were added to the pottery land, once again, as future clay reserves for use when the claypit being excavated on the west field was exhausted. In the event, the pottery was sold before the land was required for this purpose.

Premises

The potmaking and drying shed, which existed when Samuel South(1) arrived at White Hart Lane in 1886 was gradually extended over the years into a continuous building of some 30,000 square feet enclosing a rudimentary production line[1]. Raw material was delivered into the clay mill and after passing through the potmaking, drying and kiln sheds, the finished product emerged. An engineering workshop with a forge, wheelwright's shed, timekeeper's office and boiler house were incorporated within the building. Mostly, the building was of simple construction comprising a timber frame clad with corrugated iron sheeting.

Outside the main building there was a range of outbuildings, open-fronted storage sheds, garages and stables. The pottery office, a single-storey modest building, stood opposite the main entrance to the pottery. On the other side of the yard a small brick building housed the mechanism for the weighbridge installed in the yard. Used to weigh the wagons carting coal to the pottery, the weighbridge fell into disuse being unable to cope with the heavier motor lorries that were later introduced. The pottery horses were stabled in brick buildings to the rear of site having been extended on two occasions and comprising two separate blocks. The individual stalls were located either side of a central aisle. Alongside the smaller stable, pigsties were built and when the stables became redundant the smaller building was converted into a piggery. After motor transport had replaced the pottery horses an underground petrol storage tank was installed in the yard and a hand cranked pump was used to re-fuel the vehicles.

Tenants
In pre-Second World War years, parts of the pottery land were rented to tenants[1] one of whom recovered metal studs from the tyres of London taxis which were sold to the makers of rasps and files. Another tenant ground the discarded pottery "crocks" into dust which was used in the construction of hard tennis courts. Primitive machinery was employed with the belt powering the crushing rollers driven by a car raised on jacks. A third shed was occupied by a tenant who baled paper.

A decision was taken to exploit the potential income value of the land in a more organised manner and in 1938 Wood Green Council granted Samuel South & Sons permission to proceed with the erection of the first (unit 5) of seven factory units which they proposed to erect in the north-east corner of the White Hart Lane Potteries[2]. Development of the site, adjacent to the original claypit which had been filled in by that time, would have involved the demolition of the former stables and wheelwright's shop[3].

The proposed building had an area of approximately 6,600 square feet and incorporated office accommodation, a separate despatch area together with male and female washroom facilities[4]. The remaining six, smaller, units were to contain some 3,100 square feet. Each unit was to be constructed with a steel frame clad in cement and sand rendered brickwork and roofed with corrugated asbestos sheeting. A new access road to the factory estate was to be constructed and the planning proposals included provision for an extension of the roadway for further development of the site in the future.

Reference to the pottery development was made in the Borough of Wood Green Official Guide for 1939 which reported "......on land scheduled for industrial purposes, no fewer than seven factories of the single-storey type are to be erected in conformity with the Town Planning Scheme........" In the event, the development of the seven factories did not proceed,

76

presumably, because of the outbreak of the Second World War the following year.

Development of the pottery site did take place during the post war period but in a different manner to that originally proposed. Plots were leased to tenants who erected their own factory buildings on the site. Thoran Engineering Co. Ltd. were occupying premises by 1948[5] and were followed, over the ensuing years, by King & Co., Victor Sheet Metal Works, North London Store Fitting Co. Ltd., A. H. Austin & Co. and A. J. Stevens & Co. Ltd[6]. Four further tenants, F. J. & M. J. Beach, W. Steel, H & H Motors and Young & Woods occupied existing pottery buildings including the remaining stable block[7]. The construction of the factory units was not without incident. The steel framework of the building under erection for Austin was nearing completion when it collapsed and fell onto a lorry delivering materials to the site[8]. Fortunately, no-one was injured.

A local resident saw the development of light industry on the pottery site as a business opportunity and in the 1950s leased the canteen building that had been erected alongside the office during the 1930s[9]. Snacks and meals were provided not only for the pottery workforce but also the employees of the industrial estate who were the major source of income.

Middlesex Development Plan 1951[1]
When the potteries of Samuel South(1) and Edward Cole had been established in the later 19th century the surrounding area was unpopulated and planning restrictions were flexible. Seventy years later there had been substantial residential development and trades other than potmaking were being undertaken by tenants on the pottery sites. In 1951, Middlesex County Council prepared a plan for industrial and residential zoning within the County, under the Town and Country Planning Acts, which was published for public consultation.

Both pottery sites had developed broadly in a similar manner with the potmaking and kiln sheds close to the White Hart Lane frontage. Clay had been extracted towards the rear of the potteries and as each successive claypit was filled in and new pits dug the reclaimed land was available for light industrial usage. The letting of land on the Cole site seems to have developed in a more haphazard manner than that on the South property and attracted vigorous opposition from the Devonshire Hill Farm Owners-Occupiers Association whose houses abutted the rear of the Cole pottery.

The County plan permitted the continuing use of the land for clay and mineral extraction but the essential consideration was whether future, reclaimed, land should be zoned for industrial use. Because of the objections lodged against the development plan, a public enquiry was held at the Guildhall, Westminster, on 16 November 1954. South and Cole had common cause and were jointly represented at the hearing by Counsel, Mr. J. P. Widgery.

Present Site

Upon acquisition of the South pottery site in 1960, Idris Ltd. submitted planning applications to erect warehousing to provide bottling and distribution facilities, initially of 50,000 square feet, and subsequently increased to 100,000 square feet, together with office accommodation of 18,000 square feet[1]. Licence was also sought to abstract water at the rate of 50,000 gallons per day from a borehole to be sunk on the site[2]. The development proceeded but the former tenants of Samuel South & Sons remained until the expiry of their leases and the buildings occupied by them existed in 1973[3].

The premises were extended during the 1970s over the site of the last claypit and a substantial piling operation was required in order to provide adequate foundations[4]. In 1977 the site was acquired by the current owners, the Steamhouse Group, and originally used for garment manufacture and distribution[5]. Currently the warehousing is leased as self-storage units. Their website[6] claims that the facilities at White Hart Lane are "the largest single Self-storage centre in the UK". The Wonderloaf Bakery was demolished in the 1970s and replaced with a light industrial estate although the neighbouring service station survives. Idris sold the northern pottery field to the local authority and the housing in Thetford Close was built.

Operation of the White Hart Lane Pottery

Potmaking is a centuries old craft and the manufacturing processes at the pottery of Samuel South & Sons would have been instantly recognisable to a potter of any generation although powered mechanical assistance had become available.

Flowerpot

Traditionally, clay flower pots were made and ordered in 'casts' of pots. A cast was the number of pots that could be made from the equivalent volume of clay. For example, 60 x 3¼ins. diameter pots ('sixties') or 48 x 5" diameter pots ('forty-eights') could be produced from a standard ½ cwt. [25 kgs.] block of clay. In the post Second World War years it was more customary for the pots to be ordered by the thousand although some customers continued to place orders by the cast size[1].

There were regional variations in the sizes of the pots which were recommended for different plants. Samuel South & Sons offered[2]:

Number of pots to cast	Inside diameter of pot	Recommended use
60 thimbles	2"	Cacti
60 small thumbs	2 ½"	Heaths
60 large thumbs	2 ¾ "	
Small 60s	3"	
Mid 60s	3 ¼"	
Large 60s	3 ¾"	Young tomato plants
54s	4 ¼ "	
Small 48s	4 ¾ "	
Medium 48s	5"	
40s	5"	Azaleas, Hydrangeas
Large 32s	6 ¼ "	
28s	7"	Carnations
24s	7 ½	
16s	8 ½"	
12s	9 ½"	
8s	11"	
6s	12 ½	
4s	14"	
2s	15 ½"	
1s	18"	

The South pottery concentrated on '60s' and '48s' but would make a pot of any size requested by a customer. The Rooke nursery in Cheshunt, which specialised in geraniums, was supplied with a non-standard size 60 pot[3]. As the pots for this customer were thrown, the potter made a mark below the rim with his thumbnail for identification. To be profitable, the pottery depended on bulk orders for thousands of pots and, for example, the Rooke nursery purchased between 70,000 to 100,000 pots a year from Samuel South & Sons.

The highest demand for pots occurred in the spring which was the prime propagating season for the growers[4]. Some 60% of production over the remaining months was stock-piled in readiness for the seasonal demand[5]. In the event that orders for a particular size of pot were unable to be fulfilled it was the practice amongst the competing potteries to buy-in the shortfall from each other. Some limited records are available to provide details of the prices charged for the pots made by the South pottery.

Date	Cast Size	Internal diameter	Original cost	Equivalent per 1000 pots
1874[a]	60	3¼	1800 pots & £1.75	£0.97
1884[b]	Large 60	3¾"	1200 pots @ £1	£0.83
C1925[c]	Thumb	2½"	60 pots @ 4p	£0.66
1936[d]	48	5"	48 pots @ 16p	£3.33
1939[e]	Thumb	2½"	48 pots @ 11p	£2.29
1952[f]	Middle 60	3¼"	5,500 pots & £29.70	£5.40

a) Sale document – Angel Road pottery 15 February 1874
b) Sales ledger – Angel Road pottery
c) Interview with Samuel South(3) – London Evening News 16 October 1961
d) Interview with Samuel South(3) 3 January 1957 (A. W. Miller)
e) As c
f) Sales invoice 4 July 1952

Workforce
In contrast with the present trend for businesses to out-source support services, the pottery was self-sufficient from its own resources in most respects. The smithy and wheelwrights shop were always busy when horses were in use for delivery and cartage. From pot barrows to braziers, drying sheds to steam engines, clay mill to kilns, there were men within the pottery who were able to cope.

Potters	The potmakers were the elite of the pottery employees.
Wedgers	The wedgers were youths, often the sons of potters, who assisted the potmkers.
Clay workers	Clay workers excavated the claypit by hand.
Carman	Carmen drove the delivery wagons and were responsible for the well being of the horses.
Day workers	Day workers were engaged on general duties, loading deliveries and working in the drying and kiln sheds.
Bricklayer	A bricklayer was required to build and repair the kilns.
Wheelwright/ Carpenter	The wheelwright made and repaired the wheels of the wagons.
Farrier/ Blacksmith	The farrier/blacksmith shod the horses and carried out repairs to the pottery machinery
Harness maker	A harness maker repaired and maintained the harness of the delivery horses.
Stokers	The kilns required 24 hour attention when pots were being fired in order to ensure that the correct temperature was maintained.
Traveller	The traveller visited customers and obtained orders.
Office clerk	The clerk was required to record the orders, issue invoices and to enter the output of the potters so that their pay could be calculated.

The size of the workforce fluctuated and there was a marked reduction following the introduction of motor transport in 1921:

Date	Approx. No. of Employees
Circa 1895[a]	80
Circa 1918[b]	150
1939[c]	80
1957[d]	47

a) Group photograph of South employees – Bruce Castle Museum
b) Interview with Samuel South(3) London Evening News 16 October 1961
c) Interview with Samuel South(3) A. W. Miller 3 January – Bruce Castle Museum
d) As above

During the days of Samuel South(1) the rules of the company were posted in the works. Potmakers[1] and their "boy" were warned that anyone one "found aiming about the Premises", "Playing in the straw or about the clay holes" would be immediately discharged. The area around the potter's wheel was to be kept clean by "his boy" and waste clay removed. Day workers[2], paid on a hourly rate, were required to start work at 6 a.m. and lateness was penalised by deductions in pay.

The rules for the carmen[3] delivering the pots to customers were similarly strict. Stables were to be cleaned by 5.30 a.m. although those who had been on long journeys the day before and returning after 7 p.m. were able to arrive at 8.30 a.m. On Sunday attendance at the stables was required at 7 a.m. and 4 p.m. to tend to the horses but the carmen organised an unofficial rota system[4]. Instant dismissal was an optional penalty for a carman reported for either using a whip on a horse or trotting.

During the 1930s, the working hours for day workers engaged on general yard duties were 7 a.m - 5.30 p.m. Monday to Friday and to noon on Saturday with 30 minutes allowed for lunch although there were no official tea breaks[5]. In the post war period the starting time was moved to 8 a.m., lunch time increased to one hour and breaks for tea were introduced[6]. Potters' hours were slightly shorter finishing at 5 p.m. but as they were paid on piece work they were able adopt a more flexible approach to attendance[7].

None of the workforce was required to "clock in"[8]. The start and finish of working periods was signalled by a klaxon which was heard well beyond the boundaries of the pottery and was a useful reminder of the time for those living nearby. A large clock was located outside the timekeeper's office, checked against the "speaking clock" each day, and consulted by a member of the South family to ensure that the klaxon was sounded on time[9].

Long service, especially amongst the potmakers, was common and many fathers introduced their sons to the trade. In 1936, a local newspaper[10] supervised a competition to find out which of the two potteries, South or Cole, had the longest serving employees, with the following results:

Samuel South & Sons
21 longest serving employees = total of 885 years service
= 42.14 years average service

E. G. Cole & Son
21 longest serving employees = total of 891 years service
= 42.42years average service

Cole won by a narrow margin and received a silver flower pot trophy in recognition[11]. The South employees included in the assessment represented about 17% of the workforce at that time. During the course of the contest, the newspaper reported that one of the South employees had 57 years service[12] at the pottery. This means that he had started work around 1880 at the Angel Road pottery before the transfer of the business to the White Hart Lane premises in 1886.

Pay
Some glimpses of the earnings and pay structure at the pottery are possible. There was an informal arrangement between the South and Cole potteries to pay similar rates, certainly so far as the potmakers were concerned, so that earnings information of the one pottery can be applied to the other[1]. The arrangement lessened the risk of "poaching" the workers of the other pottery and prevented a potmaker playing one employer off against the other. It was, however, a complaint of the South family that their competitor did not always comply with the spirit of the understanding.

Potmakers were the skilled workmen upon whom the production of the pottery depended and their importance was reflected in the wages that they were capable of earning. Indeed, after the Second World War it was not unknown for the weekly wage of a potmaker to exceed the drawings of Samuel(3) and his brother, Charles, from the business during periods of poor cash flow (nurserymen did not have a reputation for prompt settlement of accounts). The attractiveness of the potential earnings is demonstrated by the long service of most potmakers.

In the later 1930s at least two articles appeared in the national press commenting upon the earnings available in the horticultural pottery industry. Under the headline "Fortunes from Flower-Pots", the Daily Mail[2] reported the claim that the industry was "Paying wages which rank among the highest in any industry in Great Britain" and went on to quote Sidney Cole, of E. G. Cole & Son *"The wages I am paying my men – 30s. [£1.50] per day – have not been varied since 1920, when they reached their peak following the war – despite the economy wave"*. In another article reporting on the Cole pottery, the News of the World[3] commented "The men are paid piece rates and one or two can earn as much as 4s. [20p] every hour". Again, the notes of A. W. Miller, who interviewed Samuel South(3) at length in 1957, include the following conclusion "1939 – figures of wages given me show that the competent worker was earning quite a bit above the wages of the ordinary working man in Tottenham"[4].

A daughter of a potter at the South pottery after the Second World War recalls that her father was paid ½d. [0.25p] per pot on piece-work rates[5]. Applying this rate of pay to a size '60' pot, and the output of some 1,200 pots a day for a good potter, projected over the 5½ day week suggests a weekly wage in the region of £14. The lack of knowledge about the earnings of the skilled men displayed by other employees at the potteries suggests that the potmakers kept their earnings a well guarded secret.

The yard workers were employed on a flat rate which could be supplemented with overtime. There was always a turnover of yard workers although some stayed for longer periods and many returned time and again. Bert Brown started on general yard duties at the South pottery in 1934/35 shortly after leaving school[6]. He recollects receiving 10s. [50p] a week with an extra 2s. 6d. [12.5p] for working on a Sunday morning. A local resident recalls his late brother working in the yard at the South pottery in the 1950s for a weekly sum of around £5 which was considered "a fair wage"[7]. Another former employee at the Cole pottery engaged on similar work was paid "about £6" a week[8]. He could receive a "cash in hand" payment of 10s. [50p] working for three hours on a Sunday morning with a gang of men emptying a kiln.

In earlier days, shortly before motor transport was introduced at the pottery, ordinary carmen were paid 18s. [90p] per week whilst drivers of larger wagons with 3 horses drew £1. 1s. [£1.05] plus an additional 1s. [5p] "journey" money for long distances travelled[9]. These earnings, however, could be reduced by fines levied for breach of the company rules[10]. A fine of 6d. [2.5p] could be imposed for either lateness or failing to properly clean the stable stall whilst trotting a horse attracted a levy of 1s. [5p].

In pre-Second World War days wages were paid out at midday on Saturday[11]. A company rule prohibited the payment of advances against pay (or "subs") but was not strictly enforced. Employees would queue in the pottery yard and take their turn to enter the office lobby and receive their pay packet though a sliding glass window. The potmakers (paid on piece-work) and day workers (hourly paid) would carefully check that the earnings for the past week had been correctly calculated. Wives waited outside the pottery entrance to make sure that the house-keeping money was safe before the men visited the local hostelries. Friday became the pay day after the Second World War.

Steam Engine

Main services were not laid when Samuel(1) arrived at the pottery[1] and power was required to drive the mill, potters wheels and to winch the trucks from the clay pit[2]. A steam engine provided the drive needed[3]. There was a 45 h.p. engine, with another engine of similar capacity in reserve, powered by a pair of Lancashire Boilers which were rotated at three month intervals[4]. An additional engine was installed in 1935[5] and the set-up configured so that one engine supplied power to the mill and winch, the second drove the potters' wheels with the third engine available on standby[6]. The boilers were de-scaled once a year[7]. A workman would enter the boiler and, work-ing by the light of a candle, chip away at the scale that had accumulated on the inside of the vessel[8]. The sound of the chipping resounded around the area and could be heard at River House[9]. The effect on the workman can only be imagined. Generators were installed to provide lighting[10] and, eventually, mains electricity was laid to the pottery. The steam engines were replaced by electric power after the Second World War[11].

Clay Pit

During the early years of the pottery the clay was excavated from the north and north eastern boundaries of the site[1]. These workings were filled in[2] and in April 1907 Samuel South(1) wrote to Wood Green Urban District Council offering a free shoot for 150 to 200 loads of street sweepings[3]. The offer was accepted and the arrangement continued until at least 1908[4]. Stable blocks were built and extended on the reclaimed land[5]. Extraction continued from a more centrally located pit[6] until, once again, the excavated area was filled in the 1930s[7] and works moved to the adjoining field to the west of the original pottery site[8] that had been acquired in 1915. The later pit was worked up to the closure of the pottery in 1960 and further land to the north that had been purchased for future clay stocks was never used.

Opportunities were taken to replenish clay stocks from outside sources but the operation at White Hart Lane required rather more than the material from building sites and burials[9] imported to the Angel Road pottery. The expansion of the London Underground railway system provided such opportunities. Construction of the Northern-City underground railway from Moorgate to Finsbury Park commenced in 1898 and was completed by 1904[10]. Clay from the tunnelling works was brought to the South pottery[11].

A similar opportunity arose from the excavations undertaken for the Piccadilly Line extension from Finsbury Park to Cockfosters between 1930-32[12]. No charge was levied on the contractors[13] but the Souths reserved the right to reject unsuitable loads[14], for example, clay mixed with gravel[15]. A fleet of steam lorries[16] conveyed the clay and a 24 hour inspection, organised by Charles South[17], was maintained at the pottery during tipping periods[18]. Some 100,000 cubic yards[19] were dumped at the pottery and built into a large mound[20] some 20/25 ft. high with a ramp to the top[21]. It was estimated that there was sufficient clay to make 80,000,000 flower pots[22] from the deposited clay. A further replenishment occurred in 1956 when tunnelling was being undertaken at the Lea Valley reservoirs to upgrade the London water supply[23]. Preference would be given to utilising the imported stocks before excavation of the indigenous site stock of clay.

Working outside in all weathers, the men in the clay pit had the most arduous task at the pottery. On cold winter mornings they would be given a tot of rum[24]. The London clay at White Hart Lane lay near the surface being blue/grey in appearance and turning to a light brown on exposure to the air. Excavation was undertaken in a series of steps to prevent collapse of the sides of the pit which could reach a depth of 30ft. An even working platform was created by the clayworker and the clay dug with a narrow 8" wide shovel (grafting tool)[25]. Although excavation was typically undertaken by hand, in the later years of the pottery, a mechanical drag line excavator was hired to assist with the work.

The excavated material was left to weather for several weeks in order allow the clay to crumble into smaller particles. It was necessary to keep the clay in a moist condition and to protect it with tarpaulins against either drying out in the summer or frost during the winter months. Sumps were dug to collect the water accumulating in the pit and pumped away. When ready, the weathered clay was loaded on to trucks which were winched, by a rope, up an inclined ramp on a narrow gauge railway to the mill for processing. The track of the railway was configured as necessary to reach the working area of the pit.

After the clay had been off loaded in the mill the rope was coiled in the truck which was then pushed until gravity took over. The truck descended the ramp at an alarming rate and was only arrested when the limit of the rope, which had been paying-out behind, was reached. It was not unknown for the rope to break and for the truck to career off the rails. A bell system was used to alert the workers in the pit of the truck's impending arrival. After the Second World War the steam powered winch was replaced with an electrically operated windlass adapted from a barrage balloon controller.

The railway for the last clay pit worked at the pottery crossed the site road and, without any barriers, visitors were well advised to exercise extreme caution when crossing the track. In the early 1950s the dangers of the light railway were demonstrated[26]. Two young trespassers released a truck on the ramp without the rope attached. Charles South was in the clay pit at the time and was forced to leap for safety as the truck hurtled down the track. The youths appeared at Wood Green Juvenile Court charged with wilful damage receiving a conditional discharge and ordered to pay 30s. [£1.50] damages and £1 1s. [£1.05]costs

Clay Mill
The clay mill that had been purchased from William Boulton in 1896 was in continuous use, except for the suspension of operations during the Second World War, until 1960. Arriving in the mill shed from the pit, the clay was off loaded from the truck into a hopper. A series of revolving blades thoroughly mixed the clay before dropping down to pass through two pairs of heavy rollers. Each roller, 30" long and with a diameter of 20", weighed 15 cwt. [123 kgs.]. The process was necessary to crush stones and the like that remained in the clay.

After passing through the lower pair of rollers, the clay fell into the pug mill where a further set of 36 blades rotated in a tapered cylindrical casing so that air pockets were removed and a dense clay produced as it was finally extruded through a restricted rectangular outlet. Emerging from the pug mill the clay was sliced into ½ cwt. blocks and left to stand overnight.

The following day the clay was passed again through the lower rollers which produced a more workable material ready for the potmakers. It was the responsibility of the workman at the mill to ensure that the potters were provided with a ready supply of clay.

Waste and unused clay would be returned by the potters and reprocessed through the mill[1]. Unfired pots, ("green crocks") that had been either damaged or fallen from the racks in the drying shed were collected and, after wetting, also processed again[2].

Potmaking
There were three potters' sheds, commonly referred to as the steamboard-side, pottery side and boys sheds with over 20 wheels. The latter shed was so-called because young potters were trained there. A further two wheels had been installed in the kiln shed by Samuel(2) so that retired potmakers who wanted either to visit their former colleagues or to supplement their retirement income could turn up as they pleased and continue to practise their craft[1].

The potters' wheels were arranged in lines and driven, originally, by transmission belts powered by the steam engine but later, after the Second World War, they were operated by electric motor. The arrangement of the drive mechanism was such that an individual wheel could be isolated without affecting the other wheels on the circuit[2]. In addition to the clay mill, William Boulton of Burslem had supplied the potters' machinery. The drive mechanism of the wheel, comprised two cones; an upright, idle cone and an inverted powered cone. Operation of a foot pedal brought the two cones into contact and a variable drive, capable of rapid acceleration, was transmitted to the vertical shaft supporting the horizontal wheel.

The ball of clay to be worked upon was 'thrown' on to the revolving wheel and the pot fashioned, with continuous wetting, by the application of the hand and finger pressure by the potter. Because the clay shrank during the drying and firing processes, the thrown pot was larger than the finished product. A drainage hole in the base of the pot was made with the potter's thumb. It was the boast of the South family that they could identify the maker of each pot from the unique 'fingering' made by the individual workman[3].

New employees recruited as potmakers received training and it took about six months before they were able to produce sufficient pots suitable for sale and cover their costs[4]. Only one in four of the trainees became proficient[5]. A further four to five years' experience was required to fully perfect the art of 'throwing' and be capable of producing a daily output of 1,200-1,400 pots[6]. Any of the potters in the 1936 survey who had worked at the pottery for 40 or more years, would have made, literally, millions of flower pots.

In earlier times, each potter was assisted by a 'wedger', a boy who would form (or "wedge") balls off the block of clay delivered from the mill in readiness to be thrown on the potter's wheel. The boys would also remove the boards, onto which finished pots were placed, to the drying sheds and clean the area around the wheel. They were often the sons of the potters and, in turn, trained to become potters themselves. In the later years of the pottery, their services were dispensed with, presumably because of the progressive raising of the school leaving age, and the potters became responsible for preparing the clay. Preparation time was provided between 8 a.m. and 9 a.m. when the power to the wheels was turned on[7].

The potmaker would place his 'ticket', a metal token attached to a length of cord, at the end of each board of finished pots,. The tickets were collected by the timekeeper and the daily output of the potter recorded so that his pay for the week could be calculated. Quality inspections were made by members of the South family and unsuitable pots rejected. Serious disagreements could arise because rejection would result in the potter not being paid for the pots he had made.

Drying
As the pottery business grew, the original drying shed alongside the potters' sheds did not provide sufficient space for the drying process before the pots were taken to the kilns for firing. In the 1920s a further drying shed was built on the adjoining field to the west that had been acquired in 1915[1]. Known as the 'verandahs,, there were wall shutters that could be opened to improve the circulation of air through the drying racks.

Additional space again became necessary and in 1938 planning permission[2] was granted to erect a new building which was to be the last major development at the pottery. The steel framed building was clad with rendered brickwork. Patent glazing was fitted in the pitched asbestos roof.

A series of pivoted timber sashes at ground level provided adjustable ventilation. During the wartime closure of the pottery and in the immediate post war period, the building was leased to "Superproofers", a company specialising in the waterproofing of rope. The preservative used in the treatment spread a distinctive smell around the pottery. Overflow drying racks in the kiln shed were used when the drying sheds were full but careful monitoring was needed because of the heat created by the kilns[3].

Each drying shed contained rows of timber racking in which the boards of newly thrown pots were stored to dry. Heated water pipes ran at floor level to assist the drying process which lasted between 3-5 days depending on the prevailing weather and temperature conditions. In order to prevent distortion each pot was turned at regular intervals, and then inverted, to ensure that even drying was achieved.. The process was known as 'shuffling' the pots. When suitably dried the pots were 'ranked up', placed in wheel barrows and taken to the kiln shed for firing.

Firing[1]

At the time of peak production there were six down-draught kilns enclosed within the kiln shed and a seventh outside kiln[2]. The large shed possessed a somewhat gloomy atmosphere relieved by the glow of the kiln fires and a unique mixture of the smells of the fires, coal and newly fired pots. Each domed, brick built, kiln was 10 feet in height with an internal diameter of 18 feet and a capacity for 40,000 pots. Warm air, heated by the kiln fires set in the stoke holes around the circumference of the kiln, was circulated by a system of up and down draughts controlled by the position of removable bricks in the structure of the kiln. The high temperatures, attaining 900 degrees Fahrenheit, caused the outer wall to move away from the inner wall and, although restrained by stout cast iron straps, regular rebuilding was required. Cracking caused by the thermal movement allowed cold air to enter the kiln increasing the consumption of coal in order to maintain the temperature.

Pots brought to the kilns were stacked on fire-brick shelves with the larger sizes of pot placed at the lower levels. When full, the entrance was bricked up, sealed with render and the fires lit. Vents in the kiln were left open until the steam created by the unfired pots had escaped and then closed. Kilns were fired for four to five days consuming between eight to ten tons of coal and the intensity of the fire was monitored through sight bricks set in the kiln walls. As with the drying process, weather conditions were a factor and, for example, high winds affected the draft. The kiln would be controlled to achieve a 'cherry-red' flame which indicated optimum temperature. Supervision was maintained on a 24 hour basis.

After firing, the fires were doused with salt and the kiln was allowed to cool for a further four to five days before the pots, now the familiar red colour, were removed. Premature removal from the kiln could cause the pots to crack. There was always a proportion of damaged and misfired pots that were discarded onto a pile of 'crocks' in the yard. In 1957 Walter South, recalled that Samuel South & Sons had supplied broken pots which were laid as a foundation under the pitch when 'Spurs moved to their Tottenham High Road ground in 1899[3].

After the Second World War, one of the kilns in the kiln shed was demolished and two coke boilers installed on the site. The boilers were used to heat the drying shed water pipes and were needed when the output from the Lancashire boilers used to power the steam engine was no longer available

Storage and Delivery

High sided wheel barrows were used to take the fired pots to the yard storage sheds. The yard workers were instructed not to load the barrow above the height of sides because pots could topple off but the instruction was not always followed. Motor transport superseded the horse and cart and after the Second World War there was a fleet of 4 lorries[1]. Deliveries were made within a 60 mile radius although some customers were further afield[2]. The pots were loaded on the lorries in horizontal stacks between layers of straw for protection during the journey.

Appendix 1[1]

After the death of his first wife Joseph married Mary Ann Dutton in 1869 and became the father of a further nine children. Their first child, Daniel died within six weeks of his birth in January 1871.

Florence South 1873-1912

Florence was born in Edmonton and was six months old when she accompanied her parents on the long voyage to New Zealand in March 1874. She married the Rev. David Campbell, a Presbyterian Minister. They lived in various Otago country parishes and finally in Dunback, Central Otago where Florence died in 1912. Children: Florence, Thomas, David, Eva, Joseph.

Cordelia South 1874-1897

On the voyage to New Zealand Mary Ann was pregnant with Cordelia (Nell) who was born soon after their arrival. She had a talent for sewing and worked in a clothing factory until she developed T.B. in her early 20s. After travelling to a remote Central Otago settlement, for the benefits of the climate and where her brother Moses had formerly taught, Cordelia sustained a fatal lung haemorrhage and died there soon after her arrival in her 23rd year.

Cornelius South 1887-1930

After first working at the family brickworks Cornelius (Will) moved south where he was employed as a farm labourer on a series of Southland dairy farms. By 1921 his health was poor and he lived with his brother, Ernest, and then with his sister, Evangeline, until his death in Christchurch in 1930. He never married.

Ernest South 1878-1967

Like his brothers, Ernest worked at the family brickworks, eventually buying the Walton Park business from his father in 1901. The brickfield closed in 1906. Afterwards, Ernest was for many years the caretaker of the Dunedin Botanic Gardens and the North East Valley Town Hall. He married Alice Thorn. Children: Alice, Leila, George, Charles, Clarence, Francis and Jack.

Evangeline South
Evangeline (Eva) married Frederick Ohlson, a railwayman. The family lived in Christchurch and then in Wellington. Children: Vera, Freda, Francis, Charles, Cyril.

Henry South 1882-1979
Henry (Harry) South, like his half brother Moses, did not ever work at the family brickworks. After he left school he was employed in a religious bookshop and then, after moving to Wellington, he opened the first of his South's Book Depots. These expanded rapidly throughout New Zealand as also did his chain of Times lending libraries. He was, at one time, one of the country's two leading booksellers. Harry himself was responsible for founding the Booksellers' Association of New Zealand, attending every A.G.M. for fifty years. He married Gladys Park, a daughter of a former Mayor of Dunedin, in 1910. Nine years after her death in 1957, and aged 84, Harry married Alice Corbett who also pre-deceased him. Harry lived on in good health until his death at the age of 96. There were no children.

Emalene South 1885-
In her younger days, Emalene (Lena) South played the piano at church concerts and other entertainments. She married Herbert Hogarth-Gill, a chemist, in 1908. At first they lived in a pioneering settlement in the South Catlins District of Otago although most of her married life was spent in the city of Wellington. Children: Alberta, Alfred, Essie, Cleo, Herbert, Arta.

Elizabeth South 1889-1987
Elizabeth South (Bess) was born in Dunedin, the ninth and youngest child of Joseph South's second marriage and the last of his nineteen children. Bess entered the retail trade and worked in a number of department stores until, after her marriage in 1923, she became the Buyer in the china department of a leading store, Drapery Importing Company, in Wellington. Her duties included ordering for the other branches of the chain. Bess excelled at Voice Production and won many speaking competitions, performed at concerts and read a series of historical presentations on the radio. She married Rupert Scott, a warehouse man, who later became a sales representative in Wellington and Dunedin. Child: Judith.

Appendix 2[1]

After the death of Samuel South(1) tributes were paid by the Strict Baptist community, of which he was a respected member, including the following obituary in the religious magazine, The Gospel Standard.

SAMUEL SOUTH, at Edmonton, on Jan. 2, 1919, suddenly, in his 67th year. He had been deacon since 1902 at Ebenezer Chapel, and was a lover of the glorious gospel of the Lord Jesus and His faithful servants. Often in his prayers he used the words,

"Prepare me, gracious God to stand before Thy face;
Thy spirit must the work perform, for it is all of grace."

We little thought our dear friend was to be taken from us, being the youngest of the three deacons, and doubtless were leaning very hard on him. We as a church have lost a real praying friend and miss him keenly. His wife and family have lost a loving and praying husband. At his last Sunday-morning prayer-meeting he used in his prayer in a solemn manner the words,

"Pause, my soul, and ask the question,
Art thou ready to meet God?" &c.

May his many prayers be answered that he offered on behalf of those near and dear to him by nature. "Be ye also ready, for such an hour as ye think not the Son of man cometh."

The Chapel Minutes record that a letter was sent to "Mrs. South and family" on 27 January, 1919:

At a Church meeting held on Wednesday evening last it was the unanimous wish of the Church that the Secretary write a letter to you expressing their heartfelt sympathy and condole with you in the very sad loss you have sustained by the death of your dear Kindhearted loving and praying Husband and Father.

We as a Church miss him very much and feel the loss Keenly. May the dear Lord in His infinite mercy sanctify this solemn dispensation to you all as a family and to us as a Church.

May the Lord comfort you and may your desire be to realize that your dear departed Husband and Father's God is your God and may you feel that underneath you all are [in] His everlasting Arms of love and mercy.

References

The following abbreviations are used in the references:

BCM: = Bruce Castle Museum
ELH: = Enfield Local History Unit
HL: = House of Lords Record Office
LMA: = London Metropolitan Archives
SA: = South Archive

Mention of KLB refers to the author.

Joseph South 1822-1906 p.1
[1]Tom Doig, local historian, has provided the details of the early South history
New Zealand history is based on the extensive research undertaken by Judith Cranefield, granddaughter of Joseph South.
Australian history based on information provided by Kay Shekelton, Theresa Banfield and Bryan Long, descendants of John South, Margaret Baker descendant of Henry South, and Hazel Dunn descendant of James Bysouth.
Other sources noted separately.

1822-1874 p.1
[1]Jack Wilkerson, *Two Ears of Barley*, 2nd Edition. (The Priory Press, Royston, 1970) p. 61
[2]Leone Levi *Wages and Earnings of the Working Classes*, John Murray 1885, (reprint Irish University Press 1971)
[3]1861 Census
[4]Poster in possession of Judith Cranefield

Emigration p. 5
[1]Timothy J. Hatton *Emigration from the UK, 1870-1913 and 1950-1998* University of Essex (August 2002)
[2]ibid
[3]www.theshipslist.com/Forms/assisted1869.html

The Voyage p. 8
[1]Unless separately noted the sources for this section are
Raewyn Blackstock *New Zealand Heritage* Vol. 3 part 38
Julia Millen *Colonial tears and sweat - the working class in nineteenth-century New*

Zealand (Reed, Wellington [N.Z.] 1984) pp 6-23
Judith Cranefield *Voyage of the immigrant ship "Buckinghamshire"* based on the Diary of Henry Bennewith passenger on "Buckinghamshire" March – May 1874 (see www.samuelsouth.btinternet.co.uk/voyage.htm)
www.teara.govt.nz/NewZealanders/NewZealandPeoples/TheVoyageOut/1/en
[2]Lloyd's Registry of Shipping 1875
[3]*Otago Witness* 6 June 1874
[4]ibid
[5]supra no. 2
[6]ibid
[7]supra no. 3
[8]ibid

Children p. 12
[1]The history of the lives of the children in New Zealand is exclusively based on the biographies compiled by Judith Cranefield, granddaughter of Joseph South

Ann South p. 12
[1]SA: Chris Haines, great great grandson of Ann South
[2]ibid
[3]SA: identified by Hilda Beech
[4]*Tottenham & Edmonton Weekly Herald* 17 January 1919
[5]supra no. 1
[6]ibid

Joseph South p. 13
[1]LMA: Conveyance MDR.1890/30/214
[2]LMA: Conveyance MDR.1893/16/898
[3]LMA: Conveyance MDR.1894/2/321
[4]LMA: Conveyance MDR.1896/27/849
[5]LMA: Conveyance MDR.1896/35/472

[6]ELHU: Edmonton Rates Register 1892
[7]LMA: Conveyance MDR.1895/11/663
[8]LMA: Appointment of Trustees
MDR.1906/33/204
[9]LMA: Edmonton and Tottenham
Congregational Church – Members Registers
N/C/64/13
[10]SA: William Wright mentioned in letter of
condolence 24 June 1956 on death of Samuel
South(2)
[11]*Tottenham & Edmonton Weekly Herald* 5
March 1897 and following 3 paragraphs
[12]LMA: Conveyance MDR.1898/6/359

Solomon South p. 16
[1]*Tottenham & Edmonton Weekly Herald*
Friday 17 January 1919

Samuel South(1) 1853-1919
1853-1919 p. 18
[1]SA: Last will of Samuel South(1) 23 June
1899
[2]LMA: Survey for New River Company 15
June 1870 ACC/2558/NR13/301
[3]SA: Jim South description on photograph of
Devonshire Farm house
[4]ibid
[5]LMA: Clerk's Report, Edmonton Board of
Guardians 14th November 1923: BG/E/157
[6]SA: Joan South interview with KLB 30
March 1999
[7]supra no. 5
[8] ibid & Gladys Short memories March 1996
[9]SA: Hilda Beech memories October 1984
[10]SA: Gladys Short memories 14 August 1991
[11] LMA: Conveyance: MDR.1898/6/359
[12]LMA; Conveyance: MDR.1908/11/880
[13]supra no. 10
[14]SA: Article in possession of Hilda Beech,
source not known
[15]ibid
[16]supra no. 9
[17]SA: Maud Hickson letter 15 February 1998
[18]SA: Jim South interview June 1996
[10]F. Fisk *History of the Ancient Parish Of
Tottenham* (Second Series 1923) pp 296-297
[20]SA: Gladys Short interview 19 January 1997
[21]ibid
[22]supra no. 6
[23]SA: Doris South letter 25 October 1998
[24]supra no. 9
[25]SA: Jim South letter December 1996
[26]supra no. 6

[27]SA: Jim South memories October 1996 and
remainder of paragraph
[28]*The Weekly Herald* 25 March 1904
[29]ibid
[30]*The Weekly Herald* 11 March 1904
[31]*The Weekly Herald* 30 March 1904
[32]*Enfield Observer and Local and General
Advertiser* 10 July 1903 and remainder of
paragraph
[33]SA: Edith Knight interview with KLB June
1997
[34]supra no. 9
[35]SA: Biography of Walter South by Judith
Cranefield published at
www.samuelsouth.btinternet.co.uk/wsouthnz.
htm and remainder of paragraph
[36]SA: Chris Haines e-mail 27 February 2006
[37]*Tottenham & Edmonton Weekly Herald* 10
January 1919 and remainder of paragraph
[38]*Tottenham & Edmonton Weekly Herald* 17
January 1919 and remainder of paragraph

Brickmaking p 23
[1] BCM: Lease agreement ldbcm:a/12/2/2 and
remainder of paragraph
[2]LMA: Conveyance MDR.1890/30/331
[3]LMA: Conveyance MDR.1896/45/65
[4]Kelly's London Suburban Directory,
Northern Districts, 1902
[5]SA: Joseph South, Last Will and Testament
31 January 1884
[6]LMA: Conveyance MDR.1898/6/359
[7]LMA: Mortgage MDR.1898/6/360
[8]SA: Samuel South(2) scrapbook
[9]*Wood Green Weekly Herald* 24 December
1937
[10]SA: Eric South interview with KLB 14 July
2000

Contracts p. 25
[1]BCM: Bank pass book 1882-1887
ldbcm:a/12/2/1
[2]SA: *Tottenham & Edmonton Weekly Herald*
1936 cutting in scrapbook of Samuel South(2)
[3]BCM: Tottenham Urban District Council
Minutes 1907-1911 (various)
[4]BCM: ibid 14 May 1907 p 90
[5]BCM: ibid 21 June 1909 p 188
[6]Former manorial land available for common
grazing after Lammas Day in August.
[7]BCM: Tottenham Urban District Council
Minutes 3 August 1909 p 323

[8]BCM: ibid 16 March 1909 p 986 and remainder of paragraph
[9]BCM: ibid 21 June 1909 p 188
[10]BCM: ibid 6 July 1909 p 227
[11]BCM: ibid
[12]BCM: Wood Green Urban District Council Minutes 27 March 1907 p 709
[13]ibid 25 March 1908 p 866
[14]ibid 29 April 1908 p 19
[15]ibid 24 March 1909 p 711
[16]BCM: Samuel South(3) interview with A. W. Miller 3 January 1957 852

Property and Land p. 27
[1]LMA: Appointment of New Trustees MDR.1928/43/665
[2]LMA: Conveyance MDR.1902/11/466
[3]LMA: Mortgage MDR.1902/11/464
[4]SA: Eric South letter 5 June 2000
[5]LMA: Conveyance MDR.1909/19/801
[6]BCM: Sale particulars PS 244
[7]SA: Conveyance 15 July 1912
[8]SA: Mortgage 15 July 1912
[9]SA: Conveyance 26 March 1915
[10]BCM: Tottenham Urban District Council Minutes 1915-1918 (various) and remainder of paragraph

Estate p.28
[1]LMA: Conveyance MDR.1912/11/123 [original deed in South Archive]
[2]BCM: Tottenham Urban District Council Minutes 21October 1919 p. 421
[3]LMA: Conveyance MDR.1920/27/256
[4]LMA: Mortgage MDR.1920/27/257
[5]LMA: Conveyance MDR.1920/20/18
[6]LMA: Mortgage MDR1920/20/19
[7]BCM: Tottenham Urban District Council Minutes 1921 various; LMA: MDR.1921/31/797
[8]LMA: Conveyance MDR.1921/16/702
[9]LMA: Conveyance MDR.1922/1/149
[10]LMA: Conveyance MDR.1922/30/777
[11]LMA: Conveyance MDR.1922/18/932
[12]LMA: Conveyance MDR.1923/39/119
[13]LMA: Edmonton Union Minute Book 9 October 1923 p 621 BG/E/088
[14]ibid 21 November 1923 p 747
[15]ibid
[16]EHLU: Edmonton Urban District Council Minutes 1923-1924 and 1924-1925
[17]LMA: Conveyance MDR.1925/18/345

[18]Henry Barrass was a prominent local councillor.
[19]LMA: Assignment MDR.1925/39/383
[20]LMA: Appointment of New Trustees MDR.1928/43/665
[21]SA: Eric South letter 13 March 1998
[22]ibid.
[23]LMA: Conveyance MDR.1920/27/254
[24]SA: Jim South memories October 1996
[25]SA: Joyce Barker told to KLB

South Brothers p. 32
[1]Unless otherwise stated the information in this section has been provided by Eric South, letters 13 March 1998, 21 April 1998, 5 June 2000 and interview with KLB 14 July 2000
[2]SA: Doris South letters 28 May 1998, 6 August 1998 and remainder of paragraph

Samuel South(2) 1876-1956
1876 - 1899 p. 33
[1]*Wood Green Weekly Herald* 16 September 1949
[2]*Wood Green Observer* 16 September 1949
[3]Elementary Education Act, Chapter 79, Section 5
[4]ibid Section 9
[5]supra no. 1
[6]SA: Jim South memories October 1996
[7]ibid
[8]ibid
[9]ibid & December 1996 and remainder of paragraph
[10]SA: Jim South memories March 1997
[11] ibid
[12]ibid
[13]SA: Walter Barnard letter 3 April 1997

Tottenham Terrace 1899 - 1908 p. 34
[1]SA: Joyce Barker told to KLB
[2]LMA: Edmonton and Tottenham Congregational Church – Members Registers N/C/64/11-13
[3]*Wood Green Observer* 14 September 1949
[4]SA: William Wright mentioned in letter of condolence 24 June 1956 on death of Samuel South(2)
[5]*Wood Green Weekly Herald* 16 September 1949
[6]SA: Maud South told to KLB
[7]SA: Gladys Short memories 14 August 1991
[8]BCM: *"Life and Works of William Robinson, Topographer and Historian of North-East*

London" Aleck Abraham privately published 1925, Bruce Castle Archive 790 ROB
[9]supra no. 7
[10]SA: Group wedding photograph 14 September 1899 guests identified by Hilda Beech
[11]supra no. 7
[12]ibid
[13]SA: Andy Porter Tottenham Hotspur historian letter 10 April 1997.

Snells Park 1908 - 1917 p. 36
[1]SA: Hilda Beech memories October 1984 & Electoral Register
[2]SA: Gladys Short memories 14 August 1991
[3]SA: Photograph of 39, Snells Park
[4]supra no. 2 & remainder of paragraph
[5]ibid & remainder of paragraph
[6]SA: Hilda Beech memories October 1984
[7]ibid
[8]supra no.2
[9]SA: Edith Knight interview with KLB 7 June 1997 & remainder of paragraph
[10]supra no. 6
[11]ibid
[12]supra no. 2
[13]ibid
[14]SA: William Wright letter of condolence 24 June 1956
[15]SA: supra no. 9
[16]SA: ibid & Hilda Beech memories October 1984
[17]SA: supra no. 9
[18]SA: supra no. 6
[19]SA: Gladys Short letter 3 July 1997

River House 1917 - 1926 p. 37
[1]BCM: Tottenham Urban District Council Minutes 22 March 1921
[2]ibid
[3]SA: Hilda Beech address to Edmonton Hundred Historical Society December 1976
[4]SA: Gladys Short memories 14 August 1991
[5]supra no. 3
[6]ibid
[7]SA: Maud Hickson memories November 1996
[8]Hilda Beech "South's Potteries of White Hart Lane Tottenham" in *Now Turned in to Fair Garden Plots* Occasional Paper New Series No. 45 (Edmonton Hundred Historical Society, 1983)
[9]SA: Jim South memories October 1996

[10]ibid
[11] ibid
[12]ibid
[13]supra no. 4
[14]SA: Jim South interview with KLB 17 May 1997
[15]supra no. 8
[16]SA: KLB
[17]supra no. 4
[18]supra no. 14
[19]ibid
[20]supra no 4 and remainder of paragraph
[21]SA: Joyce Barker memories December 1999
[22]supra no. 9
[23]supra no. 4
[24]ibid
[25]SA: Samuel South(2) scrapbook
[26]SA: Bert Brown interview with KLB 15 July 2003
[27]ibid
[28]supra no. 9
[29]supra no. 4
[30]SA: Joyce Barker memories January 1997
[31]supra no. 9
[32]ibid
[33]supra no. 4
[34]ibid
[35]supra no. 21 and remainder of paragraph
[36]ibid and Gladys Short letter 26 February 1998
[37]supra no. 4
[38]supra no. 21
[39]ibid and Gladys Short letter 17 January 1999
[40]SA: Gladys Short letter 17 January 1999
[41]SA: Joyce Barker told to KLB
[42]supra no. 4
[43]SA: Joyce Barker told to KLB
[44]supra no. 21
[45]SA: Maud South told to KLB
[46]SA: Gladys Short letter 31 October 1998
[47]supra no. 4
[48]SA: Joyce Barker told to KLB
[49] supra no. 21

River House 1926 - 1936 p. 41
[1]LMA: Conveyance MDR.1921/31/797
[2]LMA: Conveyances MDR.1922/1/266 & 267
[3]BCM: Tottenham Urban District Council Minutes 14 May 1926 p 97
[4]LMA: Conveyance MDR.1927/37/539
[5]LMA: Conveyance MDR.1922/1/149
[6]BCM: *The House of Whitbread* January 1929

[7]SA: Joyce Barker told to KLB
[8]BCM: Register of Deposited Plans 18 September 1934 No. 9457 p 61
[9]SA: Joyce Barker memories January 1997
[10]BCM: Register of Deposited Plans 17 July 1928 No. 8394 p 186
[11]SA: Gladys Short letter 27 September 1998
[12]SA: Jim South told to Christopher South 2004
[13]www.siddeley.com/gallery_broch01_02
[14]*"Now Turned in to Fair Garden Plots"* Occasional Paper New Series No. 45 (Edmonton Hundred Historical Society, 1983) p 49
[15]ibid; see also deposited documents in Middlesex Deeds Registry, London Metropolitan Archives
[16]LMA: Conveyance MDR.1931/40/649
[17]SA: Frank E. C. Forney letter 2 July 2002 & interview 12 July 2002 and remainder of paragraph
[18]*Wood Green Weekly Herald* 17 June 1938

River House 1936-1956 p. 44
[1]SA: Joyce Barker told to KLB
[2]ibid
[3]SA: James South memories March 1977
[4] ibid and Christopher South February 2006
[5]ibid
[6] SA: Records of Resistances Ltd. and Martin Beech; and remainder of paragraph
[7]*Wood Green Weekly Herald* 26 February 1937
[8]*Wood Green Weekly Herald* 24 December 1937
[9]ibid quotation of Edward, First Baron Thurlow 1781-1829 The Oxford Dictionary of Quotations Third Edition
[10]SA: Samuel South(2) scrapbook
[11]ibid
[12]SA: Joyce Barker told to KLB
[13]BCM: A.R.P log 1/TLA/B1/9
[14]SA: Edmonton Borough Council, Grant for Exclusive Right of Burial, no. 13585, 5 September 1949
[15]*Wood Green Weekly Herald* 16 September 1949
[16]SA: Graham South memories January 2006

Devonshire Hill Farm p. 50
[1]SA: Jim South interview with KLB 17 May 1997
[2]ibid

[3]ibid
[4]SA: Joyce Barker told to KLB
[5]SA: James South interview with KLB 17 May 1997 and remainder of paragraph
[6]SA: Hilda Beech "South's Potteries of White Hart Lane" in '*Now Turned into Fair Garden Plots*' J. G. & A. E. Robinson Edmonton Hundred Historical Society Occasional Paper No. 45 1983.
[7]ibid
[8]SA: Gladys Short Memories 14 August 1991
[9]*Wood Green Weekly Herald* 11 April 1969
[10]BCM: Wood Green Council Minutes 29 January 1930 para. 1786
[11]ibid 26 February 1930 para. 615
[12]ibid 1 October 1930 para. 1092
[13]ibid para 1605
[14]ibid para 1092
[15]ibid para. 1089
[16]ibid para. 1092
[17]LMA: Conveyance ACC/1953/C/762
[18]ibid
[19]BCM: Wood Green Council Minutes 25 July 1928 para. 767
[20]ibid para. 607
[21]ibid 26 September 1928 para. 1042
[22]LMA: Conveyance MDR.1935/24/662
[23]BCM: Wood Green Council Minutes 19 December 1934 para. 7
[24]ibid
[25]LMA: Conveyance MDR.1934/56/607

Southwold p. 52
[1]Unless otherwise stated this section is based on the memories of Joyce Barker
[2]SA: Joan South interview with KLB 30 March 1999
[3]SA: A. G. Baggot letter of condolence to Maud South 1956 (undated)
[4]*Wood Green Weekly Herald* 24 June 1938
[5]SA: Gladys Short and Joyce Barker interview with KLB January 1997
[6]supra no. 3

Angel Road Pottery
1868-1874 p. 55
[1]*"Buses in Enfield a history"* www.enfield.gov.uk
[2]*"History of Enfield Population Figures"* www.enfield.gov.uk
[3]Peter Rooke "The Lea Valley Nursery Industry", *Hertfordshire's Past* Issue 42 Autumn 1997; remainder and following paragraph

[4]Hilda Beech "South's Potteries of White Hart Lane Tottenham" in *Now Turned in to Fair Garden Plots* Occasional Paper New Series No. 45 (Edmonton Hundred Historical Society, 1983)
[5]Fred Fisk *"History of Edmonton"* (Fred Fisk, 1914) pp.136-138 and remainder of paragraph
[6]ELHU: Edmonton Rates Register 1884
[7]SA: photograph of original document (now lost)

1874-1886 p. 58
[1]ELHU: 1884 Rates register; Kelly's London Suburban Directory, Northern Districts, 1902
[2]BCM: ldbcm:a/12/2/1
[3]Leone Levi *Wages and Earnings of the Working Classes*, John Murray 1885, reprint Irish University Press 1971
[4]BCM: Samuel South(3) interview with A. W. Miller 3 January 1957 852

White Hart Lane Pottery
1886-1919 p.61
[1]BCM: Sidney Cole interview with A. W. Miller 7 January 1957
[2]BCM: Walter South & Samuel South(3) interviews with A. W. Miller 2 January 1957 & 3 January 1957
[3]BCM: Tottenham Rate Register, Lower Ward, 1886
[4]ibid
[5]BCM: Samuel South(3) interview with A. W. Miller 3 January 1957
[6]Hilda Beech "South's Potteries of White Hart Lane Tottenham" in *Now Turned in to Fair Garden Plots* Occasional Paper New Series No. 45 (Edmonton Hundred Historical Society, 1983)
[7]ibid
[8]SA: Gladys Short letter 3 July 1997
[9]BCM: photograph South workforce C1895
[10]South Archive
[11]www.thepotteries.org
[12]BCM: Samuel South(3) notes of conversation with F. Fenton 10 July 1961
[13]South Archive
[14]BCM: Inspector of Nuisances Journal ldbcm:a/1/WLA/B1/9/6
[15]BCM: Minutes of the Wood Green Local Board of Health 27 May 1897 p 464 ldbcm:a/1/WLA/A1/4

[16]Inspector of Nuisances Journal ldbcm:a/1/WLA/B1/9/6 and WLA/B1/9/7 & 8
[17]O.S. Survey 1:2500 1894 Middlesex Sheet X11.2
[18]Haringey Planning & Building Control July 1906
[19]O.S. Survey 1:2500 1913 Middlesex Sheet X11.2
[20]HL: HL/PO/PB/3/plan/1903/H23
[21]HL: HL/PO/PB/3/plan/1905/H9
[22]HL: HL/PO/PB/3/plan/1906/H13
[23]ibid
[24]SA: *Baltimore American* Tuesday March 21, 1911 "British Florists Visiting City"
[25]SA: Photograph "This photograph was taken in the Spring of 1914 on the occasion of an outing to the bulb fields in Holland by a party of nurserymen from the North London Area. My grandfather, Mr Samuel South[1] a Horticulture [sic] Pottery Manufacturer was a member of the party" Charles South
[26]SA: Peter Rooke letter 24 October 2002
[27]SA: James South interview with KLB 17 May 1997
[28]SA: Joyce Barker told to KLB
[29]BT Archives
[30]BCM: Samuel South(3) interview with A. W. Miller 3 January 1957
[31]BCM: ibid
[32]supra no. 6
[33]SA: Maud Hickson memories November 1996
[34]SA: Doris South letter 25 October 1998
[35]SA: Joan South interview with KLB 30 March 1999
[36]*Tottenham & Edmonton Weekly Herald* 17 January 1919
[37]SA: Told by Samuel(2) to grandson John Short.
[38]SA: Gladys Short Memories 14 August 1991
[39]ibid
[40]*Tottenham & Edmonton Weekly Herald* 10 January 1919

1919-1930 p. 65
[1]SA: Eric South interview with KLB 13 March 1998
[2]Hilda Beech "South's Potteries of White Hart Lane Tottenham" in *Now Turned in to Fair Garden Plots* Occasional Paper New Series No. 45 (Edmonton Hundred Historical Society, 1983)

[3]Middlesex Registration records held by Mr R G Westgate, Nottingham
[4]SA: Maud Hickson letter 4 May 1998
[5]SA: James South letter December 1966
[6]ibid
[7]SA: Joyce Barker memories 19 January 1997
[8]ibid
[9]ibid
[10]"The Lesson of the Flower Pot" *New Era Illustrated* August 1927
[11]LMA: Conveyance MDR.1915/8/454
[12]BCM: Samuel South(3) interview with A. W. Miller 3 January 1957
[13]supra no. 10
[14]SA: James South memories March 1977December 1996: Bert Brown interview with KLB 15 July 1966
[15]"A Notable Pottery – Samuel South & Sons" *The Horticultural Trade Journal* March 1938
[16]ibid
[17]SA: Maud Hickson memories March 1998
[18]supra no. 15
[19]SA: Joyce Barker memories December 1999

1930-1940 p. 66
[1]SA: Undated cutting from *Daily Mail* in Samuel South(2) scrapbook
[2]Simmons Aerofilms Ltd. SV 7163
[3]SA: Samuel South(2) scrapbook
[4]BCM; Samuel South(3) interview with Mr. Fenton July 10 1961
[5]SA: Bert Brown interview with KLB 15 July 2003
[6]The History of Atora www.atora.co.uk
[7]SA: Jim South interview with KLB 17 May 1997; Samuel South(2) scrapbook
[8]ibid
[9]BCM: Urban District Council of Wood Green Council Minutes 24 June 1931 para. 20
[10]ibid
[11]ibid 27 July para. 12 p 196
[12]ibid
[13]*Tottenham & Edmonton Weekly Herald* 20, 27 November, 4, 11 December 1936
[14]SA: G. F. Peck letter of condolence 25 June 1956
[15]SA: Bert Brown interview with KLB 15 July 2003
[16]Hilda Beech "South's Potteries of White Hart Lane Tottenham" in *"Now Turned in to Fair Garden Plots"* Occasional Paper New Series No. 45 (Edmonton Hundred Historical Society, 1983)

[17]*Wood Green Weekly Herald* 16 September 1949
[18]SA: Samuel South(3) letter to Samuel South(2) 23 March 1945

1940-1960 p. 68
[1]BCM: Samuel South(3) conversation with F. Fenton 10 July 1961
[2]ibid
[3]*London Evening News* 8 April 1947
[4]BCM: Samuel South(3) interview with A. W. Miller 3 January 1957 & remainder of paragraph
[5]SA: Joyce Barker told to KLB
[6]SA: Graham South interview with KLB June 2002
[7]ibid
[8]SA: Peter Greenall (Chris Johnson e-mail 14 February 2006) and remainder of paragraph
[9]SA: calculated from Pottery sale documents 1960
[10]SA: KLB
[11]SA: Bill Page telephone conversation with KLB 22 March 2006
[12]SA: Graham South "delivery book"
[13]Peter Rooke "The Lea Valley Nursery Industry", *Hertfordshire's Past*, Issue 42, Autumn 1997 and remainder of paragraph
[14]BCM: Samuel South(3) interview with A. W. Miller 3 January 1957
[15]ibid
[16]David Mander *Walthamstow Past* Historical Publications Ltd.
[17]SA: Chris Johnson email 26 April 2002
[18]*London Evening News* 16 October 1961.
[19]SA: Pottery sale documents 1960 and remainder of paragraph
[20]SA: Graham South memories September 2001

Pottery Site
Initial Site p. 73
[1]BCM: Tottenham Rate Register 1870: see also LMA: MDR.1869/29/206. MDR.1871/17/566-568. MDR.1871/22/145
[2]BCM: Tottenham Rate Register, Lower Ward, 1876
[3]LMA: Survey 15 June 1870 ACC.2558/NR13/301
[4]BCM: Sidney Cole interview with A. W. 7 January 1957: Hilda Beech "South's Potteries of White Hart Lane" in *'Now Turned into Fair Garden Plots'* J. G. & A. E. Robinson

Edmonton Hundred Historical Society
Occasional Paper No. 45 1983.
[5]BCM: Tottenham Rate Register, Lower
Ward, 1886
[6]HL: Plan and book of reference for proposed
Hammersmith, City & North East London
Railway HL/PO/PB/3/plan1903/H23
[7]HL: Plan and book of reference for proposed
Hammersmith, City & North East London
Railway HL/PO/PB/3/plan1905/H9
[8]LMA: Conveyance MDR.1922/5/522

West Field p. 74
[1]BCM: Tithe Map field register
[2]LMA: Conveyance MDR.1901/30/734
[3]ibid
[4]LMA: London County Council Minutes
Housing of the Working Classes Committee
Report July 1914
[4]ibid February 1915
[6]LMA: MDR.1936/23/117
[7]BCM: Wood Green Council Minutes 1935-
36
[8]*Wood Green Weekly Herald* 15 September
1961
[9]BCM: photograph and KLB
[10]supra no. 8
[11]SA: Fred Stannard memories December
2005 and remainder of paragraph
[12]BCM: Wood Green Council Minutes 1955-
56

North Field p. 75
[1]BCM: Release and Appointment D/E/31.13
[2]BCM: Earl of Dorset Survey of Tottenham
1619
[3]BCM: supra no. 1
[4]LMA: Conveyance MDR. 1928/25/748;
ACC/1953/C/762
[5]LMA: Conveyance MDR.1934/56/607
[6]LMA: Conveyance MDR.1935/24/662

Premises p. 75
[1]SA: Site plan H. Seymour Couchman & Sons
1948

Tenants p. 76
[1]SA: Jim South interview with KLB and
remainder of paragraph
[2]BCM: Wood Green Council Minutes 22 June
1938 p 260

[3]LBH: Planning Dept. TP 81A Drawing No. B
13/5 submitted by H. Seymour Couchman &
Sons
[4]ibid and remainder of paragraph
[5]SA: H. Seymour Couchman 1948 plan of
Samuel South & Sons.
[6]LBH: Planning Dept. 1957 TP 1121
Drawing B 13/17 submitted by H. W.
Couchman
[7]ibid
[8]*Wood Green Weekly Herald* 24 July 1953
[9]SA: Fred Stannard memories December 2005
and remainder of paragraph

Middlesex Development Plan 1951 p. 77
[1]Unless otherwise stated the section is based
on correspondence held at London Borough
of Haringey Planning Department

Present Site p. 78
[1]BCM: Wood Green Council Minutes 1959-
1962
[2]ibid
[3]BCM: Aerial photograph
[4]SA: Nick Clark e-mail 15 November 2001
[5]SA: Visit by KLB July 2004
[6]www.safehouse-ss.com/index2.asp

Operation of Pottery
Flowerpot p. 79
[1]BCM: Samuel South(3) interview with A. W.
Miller 3 January 1957
[2]SA: Price list (unpriced) circa 1930s
[3]SA: George Rooke telephone conversation
with KLB 29 October 2002 and remainder of
paragraph
[4]BCM: Samuel South(3) interview with A. W.
Miller 3 January 1957
[5]ibid

Workforce p. 80
[1]BCM: Samuel South & Sons "Rules for
Potmakers and Wedgers" "Rules for Day
Workers"
[2]ibid
[3]SA: Samuel South & Sons "Rules for
Carmen"
[4]Hilda Beech "South's Potteries of White Hart
Lane Tottenham" in *Now Turned in to Fair
Garden Plots* Occasional Paper New Series
No. 45 (Edmonton Hundred Historical
Society, 1983)

[5]SA: Bert Brown interview with KLB 15 July 2003
[6]SA: Graham South interview with KLB June 2002
[7]ibid
[8]supra no. 9
[9]SA: Graham South interview with KLB June 2002
[10]*Wood Green Sentinel* 25 March 1936
[11]ibid
[12]*Wood Green Weekly Herald* 12 March 1937

Pay p. 83
[1]SA: Joyce Barker told to KLB remainder and next paragraph
[2]SA: Undated cutting in scrapbook of Samuel South(2)
[3]SA: Undated cutting in scrapbook of Samuel South(2)
[4]BCM: Notes deposited by A. W. Miller January 1957
[5]SA: Christine Reed email 29 December 2002
[6]SA: Bert Brown interview with KLB 15 July 2003
[7]SA: Leslie Rodway interview with KLB December 2004
[8]SA: Frank Marden email 3 March 2006 (Dave Marden)
[9]BCM: Samuel South(3) "Notes of a conversation July 10, 1961" Mr. Fenton's account
[10]SA: Samuel South & Sons "Rules for Carmen"
[11]Hilda Beech "South's Potteries of White Hart Lane Tottenham" in *"Now Turned in to Fair Garden Plots"* Occasional Paper New Series No. 45 (Edmonton Hundred Historical Society, 1983) and remainder of paragraph

Steam Engine p. 85
[1]Hilda Beech "South's Potteries of White Hart Lane Tottenham" in *"Now Turned in to Fair Garden Plots"* Occasional Paper New Series No. 45 (Edmonton Hundred Historical Society, 1983)
[2] "A Notable Pottery: Samuel South & Sons" *The Horticultural Trade Journal* March 1938
[3]ibid
[4]ibid
[5]SA: Scrapbook of Samuel South(2)
[6]SA: Interview with Graham South June 2002
[7]SA: Interview with Jim South 17 May 1997
[8]ibid

[9]ibid
[10]supra no. 1
[11]SA: Interview with Graham South June 2002

Clay Pit p. 85
[1]O.S. Survey 1:2500 1894 London Sheet 12
[2]BCM: Walter South interview with A. W. Miller 2 January 1957
[3]BCM: Wood Green Urban District Council Minutes 29 May 1897 p 142 ldbcm:a/1/WLA/A1/16
[4]ibid 29 April 1908 p 19 ldbcm:a/1/WLA/A1/17
[5]O.S. Survey 1:2500 1913 Middlesex Sheet X11.2
[6]ibid
[7]BCM: Samuel South(3) interview with A. W. Miller 3 January 1957
[8]O.S. Survey 1:2500 1935 Middlesex Sheet X11.2
[9]supra no. 7
[10]Alan A. Jackson & Desmond F. Croome *"Rails Through The Clay"* George Allen & Unwin 1962
[11]supra no. 2
[12]supra no. 10
[13]SA: Joyce Barker told to KLB
[14]BCM: F. Fenton conversation with Samuel South(3) 10 July 1961
[15]ibid
[16]supra no. 10
[17]SA: Bert Brown interview with KLB 15 July 2003
[18]supra no. 14
[19]ibid
[20]supra no. 7
[21]supra no. 17
[22]SA: "London is Stranger than Fiction" Peter Jackson *London Evening News* 1951
[23]supra no. 7
[24]SA: Joyce Barker told to KLB
[25]supra no. 17
[26]SA: undated cutting from *Wood Green & Southgate Weekly Herald* between 1951-1953

Clay Mill p. 87
[1]SA: Bert Brown interview 15 July 2003
[2]ibid

Potmaking p. 88
[1]SA: Joyce Barker told to KLB

[2]BCM: Samuel South(3) interview with Mr. Fenton 10 July 1961
[3]Samuel South interview with *London Evening News* 16 October 1961
[4]BCM: Samuel South(3) interview with A. W. Miller 3 January 1957
[5]Charles South Interview with *London Evening News* 8 April 1947
[6]supra no. 4
[7]SA: Graham South interview with KLB June 2002

Drying p. 89
[1]"The Lesson of the Flower Pot" *New Era Illustrated* August 1927
[2]Harringey Planning Department plan no. 357A No. 13 Folio 52
[3]SA: Graham South interview with KLB June 2002

Firing p. 90
[1]Unless either wise stated the information is obtained from
"A Notable Pottery: Samuel South & Sons" *The Horticultural Trade Journal* March 1938
Samuel South(3) interview with A. W. Miller 3 January 1957
Samuel South interview with Mr. Fenton 10 July 1961

Hilda Beech notes December 1976 (probably supplied by Charles South)
Hilda Beech "South's Potteries of White Hart Lane Tottenham" in *"Now Turned in to Fair Garden Plots"* Occasional Paper New Series No. 45 (Edmonton Hundred Historical Society, 1983)
Graham South interview with KLB June 2002
[2]SA: Simmons Aerofilms SV 7163
[3]BCM: Walter South interview with A. W. Miller 2 January 1957

Storage and Delivery p. 91
[1]BCM: Samuel South(3) interview with A. W. Miller 3 January 1957
[2]SA: Graham South interview with KLB June 2002
[3]Hilda Beech "South's Potteries of White Hart Lane Tottenham" in *"Now Turned in to Fair Garden Plots"* Occasional Paper New Series No. 45 (Edmonton Hundred Historical Society, 1983)

Appendix 1 p. 92
[1]Exclusively based on the biographies compiled by Judith Cranefield, granddaughter of Joseph South

Appendix 2 p. 94
[1]The records cited are held at the Standard Gospel Library, Hove

Index

Main section on subject in **bold**. Names in *italics* refer to members of the second family of Joseph South.

May, Charles 27, 28
May, H. B. 44, 58
May, R. H. 58
Middlesex 2,
Middlesex County Council 77
Middlesex Development Plan 1951 77
Middlesex Sessions 22
Millfield Nursery 44
Moorgate - Finsbury Park Railway 86
Morrice Green 2
Mount Pleasant Road 23
Mudge, William "Billy" 35, 47

National Association of Horticultural Pottery Manufacturers 43, 48
National Emigration Aid Society 6
New River 19, 28, 37, 39, 40
New River Company 18, 50, 51, 52, 73, 75
New River House 41, 44, 46, 48, 49
New Zealand 5, 6, 7, 8, 9, 10, 11, 12, 13, 16, 17, 18, 22, 57, 93, 94
Noel Park Railway Station 65
North & East London Brick Makers Association 24, 61
North London Ballast & Sand Co. Ltd. 25
North London Store Fitting Co. Ltd. 77
Northumberland Park 15

Oak Nursery 44
Ohlson, Evangeline (b. 1880) 11 93, 94
Otago 6, 7, 10, 93, 94

Palmers Green 63, 74
Passaway, Ann 2, 3, 8, **12-13**, 16, 22
Passaway, Emma 12, 13
Passaway, Gertrude see Gertrude Burren

Passaway, John 12
Passaway, William 12, 13
Pedley, Joshua 20, 27, 28, 35
Pedley, May & Fletcher 20, 24, 27, 28, 35, 36
Pettit & Son 71
Pettit, James 2
Pettit D. & Son 42
Piccadilly Line 86
Pierce- Arrow lorry 65
Pipers Court 27, 29, 31, 39, 48
Plowman, T. 24
Port Chalmers 10
Port Melbourne 6
Poulton, G 58
Pratley, Charles 43
Primitive Methodism 3, 5, 14, 15, 20
Princes Street 13
Pymmes Brook 56

Ragnells Field 75
Raylands Field see Ragnells
Read, Roland 49
Rectory Farm 38
Reed 1
Regent Garage 74
Relieving Officer 29
Resistances Ltd. 44
Rickett (coal merchant) 62
River House 28, 29, **37-44**, 85
River Terrace 42
Rix, Albert 15
Rix, Florence Ellen 13, 14, 15, 35, 57
Robinson, Dr. William 35
Robinson, William jnr. 35
Rooke Nursery 80
Rooke, George 59, 64
Rooke, Peter 64
Rotary Club of Wood Green 44, 45, 48, 49
Sankey, Richard 43, 61, 62, 68, 69, 73

108

South, Mary Ann (second wife of Joseph South) 3, 4, 5, 8, 9, 10, 11, 12, 13, 18, 56
South, Moses (b. 1867) 2, 8, 9 **17**
South, Peter (b. 1935) 48, 69
South, Samuel (b. 1817) 1
South, Samuel(1) (b. 1853) 2, 3, 8, 12, 16, **18-32**, 33, 57, 58, 60, 61, 64, 74, 75, 77, 81, 85, 95
South, Samuel(2) (b. 1876) 13, 14, 18, 21, 28, 30, 31, **33-53**, 64, 65, 66, 67, 69, 70, 75
South, Samuel(3) (b. 1909) 37, 44, 46, 47, 48, 49, 61, 66, 68, 69, 70, 71, 74, 83
South, Sarah (b. 1835) 1
South, Sarah 12, 13, 14, 15, 24
South, Solomon (b. 1851) 2, 3, 8, 12, **16**, 55
South, Thomas (b. 1832) 1
South, Walter (b. 1881) 18, 30, 32, 64, 65, 91
South, Walter, (b. 1857) 2, 8, 9, **16-17**, 22
Southgate 1, 44, 63
Southwold 44, **52-54**
Sperling, Henry 38
St. James Church of England School 36
St. Loys Road 32
Standon 2
Steamhouse Group 78
Steel, W 77
Stevens. A. J. & Co. Ltd. 77
Stockbridge (coal merchant) 62
Strawbridge, R. Ltd. 74
Strict Baptists 20, 23, 95
Stye Field see Sly Field
Superproofers 90
Sydney (Aus.) 16, 22

Taylor, Walker & Co. Ltd. 29
Tent Farm 73

Tentdale 18
Thetford Close 78
Thoran Engineering Ltd. 77
Tithe Map 1844 38
Tompkins, Charles 45, 48, 49, 53
Tottenham 12, 15, 18, 23, 27, 32, 35, 36, 38, 55, 59, 64 , 73, 84
Tottenham High Road 19, 34, 36, 47
Tottenham Hotspur 28, 36, 47, 91
Tottenham Potteries 63
Tottenham Terrace **34-36**
Tottenham Urban District Council 25, 26, 28, 29, 38, 39, 41, 44
Trafalgar House 35
Tuck, G & A 45, 69, 71
Tuck, Arthur 45
Tyler, J 58

Union Road 34

Victor Sheet Metal Works 77

Waltham Cross 71
Walton Park (NZ) 11
Ward of Darleston (pottery) 43, 68
Ware 2, 6, 13
Water Lane see Angel Road
Waton, Rev. C. F. 49
Webb, Sarah see Sarah South
Webb, William 13, 14
Wedlake, Saint & Co. 71
Weir Hall 38
Welfare Brothers 35
West Green, Tottenham 5, 14, 45
Whitbread & Co. Ltd. 36, 42, 65
White Hart Lane 18, 20, 23, 28, 35, 38, 39, 48, 49, 60, 61, 63, 67, 73, 74, 77
White Hart Lane Pottery 12, 20, 22, 28, 30, 35, 48, 60, **61-72** (History), **73-78** (Pottery Site), **79-92** (Operation of Pottery)
White Hart Public House 39, 42, 48